ABUSIVE RELATIONSHIPS
AND DOMESTIC VIOLENCE

By Jennifer Lombardo

LUCENT
PRESS

Published in 2019 by
Lucent Press, an Imprint of Greenhaven Publishing, LLC
353 3rd Avenue
Suite 255
New York, NY 10010

Designer: Deanna Paternostro
Editor: Jennifer Lombardo

Library of Congress Cataloging-in-Publication Data

Names: Lombardo, Jennifer, author.
Title: Abusive relationships and domestic violence / Jennifer Lombardo.
Description: First Edition. | New York : Lucent Press, [2019] | Series: Hot
  topics | Includes bibliographical references and index.
Identifiers: LCCN 2018030681 (print) | LCCN 2018031957 (ebook) | ISBN
  9781534565135 (eBook) | ISBN 9781534565128 (library bound book) | ISBN
  9781534565111 (pbk. book)
Subjects: LCSH: Offenses against the person. | Interpersonal
  relations–Psychological aspects. | Family violence.
Classification: LCC HV6493 (ebook) | LCC HV6493 .L66 2019 (print) | DDC
  362.82/92–dc23
LC record available at https://lccn.loc.gov/2018030681

Printed in the United States of America

CPSIA compliance information: Batch #BW19KL: For further information contact Greenhaven Publishing LLC, New York, New York at 1-844-317-7404.

Please visit our website, www.greenhavenpublishing.com. For a free color catalog of all our high-quality books, call toll free 1-844-317-7404 or fax 1-844-317-7405.

CONTENTS

Adolescence is a time when many people begin to take notice of the world around them. News channels, blogs, and talk radio shows are constantly promoting one view or another; very few are unbiased. Young people also hear conflicting information from parents, friends, teachers, and acquaintances. Often, they will hear only one side of an issue or be given flawed information. People who are trying to support a particular viewpoint may cite inaccurate facts and statistics on their blogs, and news programs present many conflicting views of important issues in our society. In a world where it seems everyone has a platform to share their thoughts, it can be difficult to find unbiased, accurate information about important issues.

It is not only facts that are important. In blog posts, in comments on online videos, and on talk shows, people will share opinions that are not necessarily true or false, but can still have a strong impact. For example, many young people struggle with their body image. Seeing or hearing negative comments about particular body types online can have a huge effect on the way someone views himself or herself and may lead to depression and anxiety. Although it is important not to keep information hidden from young people under the guise of protecting them, it is equally important to offer encouragement on issues that affect their mental health.

The titles in the Hot Topics series provide readers with different viewpoints on important issues in today's society. Many of these issues, such as domestic abuse and free speech rights online, are of immediate concern to young people. This series aims to give readers factual context on these crucial topics in a way that lets them form their own opinions. The facts presented throughout also serve to empower readers to help themselves or support people they know who are struggling with many of the challenges adolescents face today. Although negative view-points are not ignored or downplayed, this series allows young people to see that the challenges they face are not insurmount-able. Abusive relationships can be ended, the internet can be navigated safely, and the environment can be saved.

Quotes encompassing all viewpoints are presented and cited so readers can trace them back to their original source, verifying for themselves whether the information comes from a reputable place. Additional books and websites are listed, giving readers a starting point from which to continue their own research. Chapter questions encourage discussion, allowing young people to hear and understand their classmates' points of view as they further solidify their own. Full-color photographs and enlight-ening charts provide a deeper understanding of the topics at hand. All of these features augment the informative text, helping young people understand the world they live in and formulate their own opinions concerning the best way they can improve it.

Understanding Abuse

Domestic violence, or physical abuse, seems straightforward on the surface: If one partner in a romantic relationship physically hurts another—for instance, by punching or slapping them—that is abuse. Few people would argue with this definition. However, things start to get more complicated when abuse is explored more deeply.

When confronted with the realities of abuse by someone they know personally—for example, if someone is friends with a couple and one of them says the other is being abusive—some people will deny it could be possible or will make excuses for the behavior. An abused person may hear things such as, "It was just one time," "I know him; he wouldn't do that," or "Did you do something to make him mad?" Because abuse is considered such a terrible act in most societies, some people have difficulty coming to terms with the fact that someone they know and like is not as nice as they might have thought. Added to this is the fact that abusers often seem charming, generous, and nice in public, creating a huge disconnect between the way most people see them and the way their partner describes how they act in private.

For example, in 2016, actor Johnny Depp was accused of domestic violence by his ex-wife, Amber Heard. She had evidence, including photographs of her injuries, to back up her claim, and Depp's former managers filed documents in court stating that they had witnessed the abuse. However, even with all this evidence, many people believed Heard was lying to get money from Depp because they were unwilling to believe that an actor

Johnny Depp has faced allegations of abusing his ex-wife Amber Heard, and she took photos to back up her accusations. However, many of his fans and people who have worked with him were unwilling to believe it could be true. As a result, Depp's career has not suffered.

they loved in movie franchises such as *Pirates of the Caribbean* and *Fantastic Beasts* could do something so horrible.

Even when an abuser is not a personal friend or a beloved celebrity, emotional abuse is often not treated seriously. Many people deny that it exists or that it is a serious problem, and it is often subtle enough that even the person being abused questions if it is actually abuse. As abuse expert Lundy Bancroft pointed out,

Women can find it difficult not to blame themselves for their reactions to what their partner does if they don't even know what to call it. When someone slaps you in the face, you know you've been slapped. But when a woman feels psychologically assaulted, with little idea why … she may turn her frustration inward. How do you seek support from a friend, for example, when you don't know how to describe what is going on?[1]

Although emotional abuse does not leave physical scars, it can be just as devastating to a person's emotional and mental health as physical abuse. It can also be harder to escape, as emotional abuse victims have a more difficult time acknowledging that the abuse is happening and getting others to believe it.

WHAT WE SAY

"We say these women are almost always liars,
that they weren't really hurt, that they're just trying to destroy
innocent men. Statistically, that's almost never true,
but we say it anyway."

—Constance Grady, journalist

Constance Grady, "Amber Heard Did What Abuse Victims Are 'Supposed' To Do. People Still Didn't Believe Her," Vox, August 22, 2016. www.vox.com/2016/8/19/12555646/amber-heard-johnny-depp-domestic-abuse-divorce.

When Is It Abuse?

Talking about abuse is also difficult because many people tend to think in absolute terms. For example, someone may say that any time a person hits another person, it is abuse. This may lead someone who hits their partner purely by accident—such as by opening a door too fast without realizing someone was on the other side—to fear that people may think they are an abuser. Additionally, many people do things to hurt others emotionally without meaning to. For example, someone may get angry at their partner and yell during an argument. Afterward, the person who was yelled at may question whether they were the victim of abuse.

It is difficult, if not impossible, to come up with a one-size-fits-all definition of abuse; often, things need to be looked at in a situational context. Most people think of abuse as occurring within a romantic relationship, but friendships can be abusive as well, and children as well as elderly people are frequently the victims of abuse by family members and other caretakers. Name-calling can be abusive, but if two friends call each other names as a joking sign of affection and neither is upset by it, it would be difficult to call that abuse. Yelling can be a sign of an abusive relationship, but if someone loses their temper, raises their voice, and later sincerely apologizes and makes a noticeable effort not to do it again, that is generally not considered abusive behavior, either. Most people have yelled at some

*Pushing or shoving is sometimes considered abuse, but other times,
these actions happen when people are playing and having fun together.
In those cases, the behavior is not considered abusive.*

point in their life, and it is considered a normal expression of emotion.

In an article for *Psychology Today*, counselor Andrea Mathews addressed some things that are often mistaken for emotional abuse:

> It is not emotionally abusive to break up with a partner. It is not emotionally abusive to argue with your partner. It is not emotionally abusive when someone reacts to what you have done with hurt. People react out of their own perceptions, so their reactions do not define your behavior. It is also not emotional abuse to speak one's mind with blunt honesty. Perhaps the statement lacks tact, but it is not emotionally abusive. Again, just because someone reacts to what has been said with hurt does not mean that one has been emotionally abused.[2]

The biggest indicator of abuse, according to Mathews, is control. This can apply to both verbal and physical abuse. When someone uses their words or actions to force another person to behave a certain way and does not take that person's feelings about it into account, it is likely abuse. The abuser may be acting this way deliberately, or they may not even realize that what they are doing can be considered abuse. Some people, Mathews said, are emotionally abusive because they are insecure in the relationship and want the other person to behave in a way that makes them feel better. Others may genuinely think they know what is best for their partner and order their partner to do things they do not want to do out of a feeling of concern for them. However, the reasoning does not matter; what matters is that another person is being harmed, either mentally or physically, by this controlling behavior.

Abusers often do not engage in every single type of abusive behavior. However, abusers are often a combination of physically and emotionally abusive. Some may be purely emotionally abusive, but rarely is someone purely physically abusive. This variety in the way abuse is performed can be confusing for victims as well as others who witness the abuse. Understanding what is abuse and what is not—and how to deal with abusive as well as hurtful but nonabusive situations—is essential for creating healthy friendships, romantic relationships, and family dynamics.

CHAPTER 1

Physical Abuse

Physical abuse has an unfortunately long history around the world. Physical abuse of a spouse was not made illegal in the United States until 1920, and it was rarely taken seriously by police until the 1970s. Before that time, abuse of a wife or child was often seen as justified, especially if the wife or child was doing something men did not consider acceptable, such as questioning their decisions or "talking back." Police and neighbors tended to turn a blind eye when they witnessed abuse, believing it to be a private family matter in which they had no business getting involved.

However, some people throughout history have been willing to take a stand against abuse. A widespread myth says that the phrase "rule of thumb," which refers to a guideline for doing something, came from an old British law saying that a man could beat his wife with anything that was less than the width of his thumb. Researchers trying to verify this myth found evidence from 1782 of a judge who stated that domestic violence should be allowed but was criticized by some of the British public for it, showing that some British people at that time spoke out against abuse. Today, that opposition has increased, and people have become more likely to step in when they see or hear incidents of domestic violence. However, many misconceptions about physical abuse persist.

How Widespread Is Abuse?

Exact figures on abuse are difficult to find because many victims suffer silently instead of reporting the abuse. Some do this because they are afraid they will be killed if they speak up; others have been convinced by their abuser that they deserve the abuse or caused it to happen through something they did or said—or did not say or do. Many abuse victims blame themselves and look for ways to avoid triggering an attack. However, since the reality is that abuse is the abuser's fault and never the victim's, it is generally impossible for the victim to behave "correctly;" an abuser will always find a reason to continue the abuse. As Bancroft noted, "abuse is not a product of bad relationship dynamics, and you cannot make things better by changing your own behavior or by attempting to manage your partner better. Abuse is a problem that lies entirely within the abuser."[3]

The way statistics are tracked also presents confusion. In 2014, the Bureau of Justice Statistics, which is part of the U.S. Department of Justice, reported that nonfatal domestic violence incidents had decreased 63 percent between 1994 and 2012, "from 13.5 victimizations per 1,000 persons age 12 or older in 1994 to 5.0 per 1,000 in 2012."[4] Some people attributed this to the increase in awareness of domestic violence, while others said it was due to the increase in options for victims, such as more women's shelters. However, many groups that work directly with victims of domestic violence and abuse say they have seen an increase in the number of people looking for help. This means that fewer people may be getting arrested for domestic violence according to the Bureau of Justice Statistics, but the number of people being abused may be increasing or holding steady. According to the National Network to End Domestic Violence (NNEDV), 88 percent of the programs it offers to help victims have seen an increase in the number of people seeking assistance. One reason for this difference in statistics may be that more women are seeking help and choosing not to press charges. Additionally, the Bureau of Justice Statistics only tracks physical abuse, not emotional abuse.

Although the specific numbers are unclear, what is undebatable is that abuse is a serious problem in the United States as well as many other countries around the world. Domestic partner violence is the leading cause of injury for women in the United States, and the Centers for Disease Control and Prevention (CDC) reported in 2016 that 20 people are abused by a partner every minute. The CDC also conducted a study of domestic violence in 18 states between 2003 and 2014. In these states, nearly half of all the women murdered each year were killed by a romantic partner. Other research has shown that young women between the ages of 16 and 24

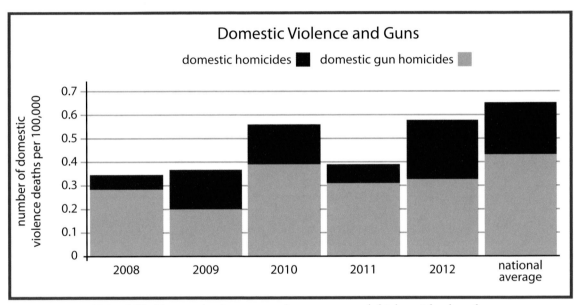

Domestic Violence and Guns

domestic homicides ■   domestic gun homicides ▨

y-axis: number of domestic violence deaths per 100,000

x-axis: 2008, 2009, 2010, 2011, 2012, national average

Being killed by an abusive partner becomes a much higher risk when the abuser has access to a gun, as this information from the Connecticut Mirror— *based on statistics for Connecticut from the Federal Bureau of Investigation (FBI)—shows.*

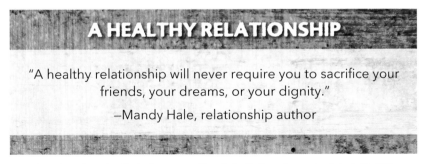

A HEALTHY RELATIONSHIP

"A healthy relationship will never require you to sacrifice your friends, your dreams, or your dignity."

–Mandy Hale, relationship author

Quoted in Samantha Gluck, "Quotes on Abuse," HealthyPlace, last updated April 29, 2018. www.healthyplace.com/insight/quotes/quotes-on-abuse/.

are the most likely to experience domestic violence from a romantic partner.

Can Men Be Abused?

Because so many statistics and other information about abuse focus on women, many people wonder: Can men be abused? The answer is yes, although women experience abuse at much higher rates than men and it is considered much more of a problem for women than for men. Some people say men cannot be abused, and when a man speaks out about being abused, he often risks being mocked, especially if his abuser is a woman. Since society often thinks of women as weaker than men and since emotional abuse is often ignored, people may say a man should be able to fight off a woman who is attacking him. Some people feel that this kind of reaction leads men to fear reporting abuse because they might not be taken seriously. People who feel this way often believe men

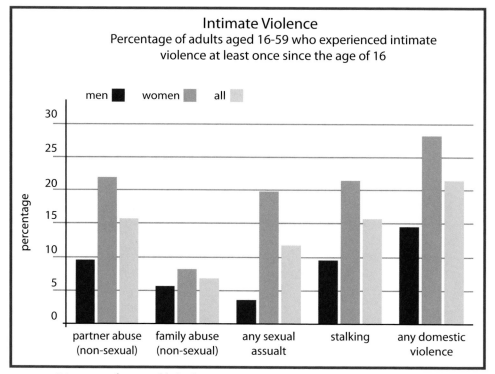

Women are far more likely than men to experience some form of abuse, as this information from the Department of Justice shows.

are victims far more than people think; some groups say that up to 40 percent of abuse victims are male, and this statistic has been repeated by some news outlets.

However, most experts question the methods by which these groups calculated that percentage. According to Bancroft, who has worked directly with abusers for more than 15 years, not only is abuse more commonly directed at women, it also often has a much more devastating effect on their lives. While it can certainly be embarrassing and scary for a man to come forward and report his abuse, Bancroft said, women feel the same embarrassment, yet report far more often or have others report on their behalf when they notice bruises or hear yelling and other sounds of violence coming from a neighbor's house. If being questioned about the truth of abuse stopped all victims from coming forward, women would not report either, as they often face disbelief as well. Bancroft noted,

> There are certainly some women who treat their male partners badly, berating them, calling them names, attempting to control them. The negative impact on these men's lives can be considerable. But … If there were millions of cowed, trembling men out there, the police would be finding them. Abusive men commonly like to play the role of victim, and most men who claim to be "battered men" are actually the perpetrators of violence, not the victims.[5]

Abusive men commonly claim to be abused themselves when their victims fight back. In reality, this is self-defense, not abuse. Additionally, sometimes the misunderstanding of what can be considered abuse comes into play. Researcher Elspeth McInnes, who interviewed men who claimed to be victims of abuse, said some of the interviewees considered not coming home to a hot meal and women spending too much money on shopping to be forms of abuse. "Women were talking about being run over, being drugged and raped at knifepoint, having their children dangled over high rise balconies till they did as they were told and of course you get verbal and emotional violence," said McInnes. "When we were talking about physical violence against men, one of the worst examples was that she banged his head with the cupboard door—which isn't good—but the sheer level of fear, harm and terror that women talked about was simply not present in what the men's data showed."[6]

THE DANGER OF "BOYS WILL BE BOYS"

"We cannot hand over a free pass for hurting others—and that's exactly what happens when people say 'boys will be boys.'"

—Jennifer Hicks, *Huffington Post* blogger

Jennifer Hicks, "Stop Saying 'Boys Will Be Boys,'" *Huffington Post*, October 16, 2014. www.huffingtonpost.com/jennifer-hicks/stop-saying-boys-will-be-boys_b_5979416.html.

Bancroft believes that since abuse is about a power imbalance, it is difficult—but not impossible—for women to abuse men in a patriarchal society where men traditionally hold much more power. In Western society, men have more privilege than women; for instance, when a man tells someone what to do, he is often considered to be a natural leader, while a woman who tells people what to do is generally seen as nagging or bossy. This type of privilege, according to Bancroft, is key to defining abuse because it naturally gives men more power in society. White people also have more privilege than people of color, so a white man has two forms of privilege working for him, while a woman of color has two forms working against her. Bancroft does note, however, that when two men or two women are in a relationship, it is possible for one of them to abuse the other even though this gender-based power imbalance is not present.

It is difficult to prove or disprove Bancroft's theory with statistics. In 2013, the National Domestic Violence Hotline reported that 13 percent of the calls it received were from men, and the CDC reports that one in seven men ages 18 and up are victims of domestic violence in their lifetime, compared with one in four women. However, these numbers do not break down which men have been abused by women and which have been abused by other men. All that is certain is that men are not immune to this problem. Also, since abuse affects women much more frequently, it can be more difficult for men to find help.

*Abuse can happen within same-sex relationships
even though there is no gender-based power imbalance.*

Identifying Physical Abuse

Some physical abuse is easy to identify. Someone who has been punched, slapped, kicked, or otherwise beaten is aware of what has just happened, although they may later try to rationalize it away. However, sometimes people are unaware that what has happened to them can be considered physical abuse. They may believe it is not serious if it does not leave a mark or break the skin. Abusers tend to reinforce this view by saying things such as, "Don't be dramatic, I didn't even hit you that hard." It is not uncommon for abused women to adopt this view, making it hard for them to see themselves as abuse victims.

Physical abuse does not have to leave a mark or even hurt to be considered abuse. The main thing is that the physical contact is unwanted and continues after the person has asked for it to stop. In some cases, the abuser does not even have to touch the other person; the threat of violence is enough. The following things are considered examples of physical abuse:

- *Scratching, punching, biting, strangling or kicking.*
- *Throwing something at you such as a phone, book, shoe or plate.*
- *Pulling your hair.*
- *Pushing or pulling you.*
- *Grabbing your clothing.*
- *Using a gun, knife, box cutter, bat, mace or other weapon.*
- *Smacking your bottom without your permission or consent.*
- *Forcing you to have sex or perform a sexual act.*
- *Grabbing your face to make you look at them.*
- *Grabbing you to prevent you from leaving or to force you to go somewhere.*[7]

Physical abuse can also include withholding certain items, such as refusing to let a partner get dressed so they are unable to leave the house or denying them access to the bathroom, as well as physically restraining them—for instance, by locking them in a room. Sexual abuse is related to physical abuse and includes things such as taking off a condom during sex without the other person's consent, forcing someone to take nude photos, and kissing or touching someone after the person has asked them to stop.

Threatening harm can also be considered physical abuse, even if the threat is never carried out. For instance, raising a fist as if preparing to hit, standing very close and yelling, making verbal threats of performing violent acts with a weapon, or being violent with inanimate objects—for example,

An action can be physically abusive even if the abuser never touches the victim. Actions such as punching holes in a wall, breaking the victim's personal possessions, and raising a hand in a threatening way are considered physically abusive because they make the victim fear for their physical safety.

punching a wall or breaking items that belong to the victim—are all considered by many to be forms of physical abuse, even though the abuser never touches the victim.

According to Bancroft, abusers often consider their own tactics to be justified and will not see them as abuse, but they will frequently condemn other abusers' tactics as abuse if they are different from their own. For instance, a man who will only slap his partner might be horrified by a man who uses an improvised weapon, such as a belt. Abusers often do only what they consider morally acceptable; they know other people will look down on them, which makes them hide their actions, but in their minds, they always have a good reason for what they did. Bancroft stated that this shows that "an abuser's core problem is that he has a distorted sense of right and wrong."[8]

Making Excuses

Many people who are on the receiving end of domestic violence do not want to believe it is happening to them. They

#WhyIStayed

Some people are confused about why abuse victims rationalize what has happened to them by saying things such as, "He didn't mean it," "I made him angry," or "It was just one time." It is common to hear people question why a woman would continue to stay in an abusive relationship. In 2014, National Football League (NFL) running back Ray Rice was caught on camera assaulting his fiancée Janay Palmer in an elevator. When Palmer later married Rice, some people wondered why she did not leave the relationship instead. In response, the hashtag #WhyIStayed went viral on social media, with domestic violence victims sharing their stories. Some of the reasons included:

- *I tried to leave the house once after an abusive episode, and he blocked me. He slept in front of the door that entire night.*

- *He said he would change. He promised it was the last time. I believed him. He lied.*

- *I had to plan my escape for months before I even had a place to go and money for the bus to get there.*

- *Because he made me believe no one else would understand.*

- *My mom had 3 young kids, a mortgage, and a PT [part-time] job. My dad had a FT [full-time] paycheck, our church behind him, and bigger fists.*

- *because my word was the only evidence.*

- *b/c [because] he never hit me and I didn't think verbal abuse and emotional manipulation was considered an abusive relationship.*

- *Because after being stuck in an abusive relationship for awhile I started to believe I deserved all of it.*

- *because I was 15 and he said he loved me and I didn't know what love was. I thought I had to marry him. It was my fault.*[1]

Some of these tweets show the way an abuser makes a victim blame themselves. Although an abuse victim may feel as though the abuse is their fault, the true blame always lies with the abuser.

---

1. Quoted in Jared Keller, "19 #WhyIStayed Tweets That Everyone Needs to See," *Mic*, September 8, 2014. mic.com/articles/98326/19-why-istayed-tweets-that-everyone-needs-to-see#.bemKThgl4

love the person they are dating or married to, so it is difficult for them to understand that someone who claims to love them back could hurt them that way. They may try to convince themselves that their loved one did not mean to do it. Common examples of this way of thinking are that the person was so upset or overcome with love that they lost control, is simply bad at expressing their feelings in healthy ways, has a mental illness that makes them unable to control their actions, was abused as a child or saw their mother abused and has learned unhealthy behaviors, was "ruined" by a previous unhappy relationship in which they were cheated on or otherwise emotionally hurt, has a temper problem, has a substance abuse problem that causes them to be abusive toward their partner, or feels powerless in other parts of their life (such as at work or school).

The idea that abusers are not in control of their actions is false, although it is one that abusers like to promote, as it helps them feel justified in their actions and makes it easier for their victims to forgive them and stay with them. Bancroft noted that he busted the myth of an abuser who lacks control by asking his clients—abusive men who entered Bancroft's counseling program to help them change their behavior—what stopped them from killing or more seriously injuring their partner during an abusive episode:

> For example, I might say, "You ... grabbed the phone out of her hand and whipped it across the room, and then you gave her a shove and she fell down. There she was at your feet, where it would have been easy to kick her in the head. Now, you have just finished telling me that you were 'totally out of control' at that time, but you didn't kick her. What stopped you?" And the client can always give me a reason.[9]

Trying to keep the fight from getting loud enough to alert someone who might intervene, fear of seriously injuring or killing their partner, or fear of being arrested are all reasons why an abuser might choose to stop themselves from going further. The fact that they can make that choice proves that they are fully in control of their actions.

Sometimes people say there is a reason why an abuser cannot control themselves, such as a mental illness or substance use disorder. These, too, are only excuses. Not all abusers have a mental illness or a substance use disorder, and not all people with one or both of these issues are abusive. While the presence of one of these issues often makes the abuse worse, it does not cause abuse. This can be proven by the fact that most abusers only abuse certain people, such as their partners or children. This shows that they are able to control themselves in certain situations. According to Bancroft,

> *a small percentage of abusers—perhaps one in twelve—may have psychological conditions such as narcissistic or borderline personality disorder, in which they literally block any bad behavior from consciousness. One of the clues your partner may have such a disturbance is if you notice him doing similar things to other people. If his [actions] are restricted to you, or to situations that are related to you, he is probably simply abusive.*[10]

Although drugs and alcohol often make abuse worse,
experts say they do not make a person abusive.

Another common excuse used by both abusers and their victims is that the abuser is unhappy for some reason. However, this, again, is just an excuse; many people who are unhappy learn to control their emotions rather than taking them out on the people around them. Abusers might also claim that they learned this behavior from their home environment while growing up. Research has shown, though, that men who come from abusive backgrounds are not more likely to abuse women, although they are more likely to act violently toward other men.

Masters of Manipulation

It can be difficult to spot an abuser right away. Most abusers are charming and charismatic; they trick their victims into thinking they are nice, and even after they become abusive, many outsiders have a difficult time believing it because the abuser continues to put on a show. They often know exactly how to manipulate people. In one example, Bancroft mentioned a client in his program who consistently made statements about how much he was learning about himself, causing Bancroft to believe that he was willing to work on his abusive attitudes. However, when Bancroft talked to the

ABUSE IS NOT LOVE

"The confusion of love with abuse is what allows abusers who kill their partners to make the absurd claim that they were driven by the depths of their loving feelings. The news media regrettably often accept the aggressors' view of these acts, describing them as 'crimes of passion.' ... Genuine love means respecting the humanity of the other person, wanting what is best for him or her, and supporting the other person's self-esteem and independence. This kind of love is incompatible with abuse and coercion."

–Lundy Bancroft, abuse expert

Lundy Bancroft, *Why Does He Do That?: Inside the Minds of Angry and Controlling Men*. New York, NY: G.P. Putnam's Sons, 2002, p. 65.

client's wife, she told him that her husband always came home from the sessions angry, and he took that anger out on her by physically abusing her; he was ordered by the court to attend the program after serving jail time for abuse, and he blamed his wife for calling the police on him. This shows that abusers know what to do and say to fool even experts into thinking they are not abusive.

Abusers make an effort to be charming and nice in public so it is harder for others to believe the accusations against them.

Warning Signs

Not all abusers become violent, but there are some warning signs that someone who is already engaging in emotional abuse will escalate to abuse that can cause physical harm. These include:

- using violent gestures when angry, such as throwing things or ripping their own clothes
- becoming angry when asked to stop doing things their partner considers frightening
- blaming their partner for their own violent actions

Physically Abusive Friendships

Although people are far more familiar with abuse that happens within family or romantic relationships, friendships can be abusive as well, both emotionally and physically. Just like in other abusive relationships, one person tries to control another and does not take the feelings of the other person into account. One example given by Kai Cheng Thom in an article for *Everyday Feminism* was a "codependent best friendship I developed with a … person who refused to accept 'no' for an answer when I couldn't or didn't want to hang out, and would punch me—hard enough to bruise—to show 'how much I was hurting him.'"[1]

Some signs of a physically abusive friendship include:

- One person is constantly afraid for their safety but does not feel as though breaking off the friendship is an option.

- One person is too scared to be their true self around their friend because acting a certain way "causes" abuse.

- The abuser believes they are allowed to hit their friend and also believes their friend should not defend themselves.

- One friend regularly touches the other inappropriately or nonconsensually and refuses to listen to requests to stop.

- One friend finds themselves consistently making excuses for the other friend's behavior, such as, "They only hit me when I make them mad."

Physical abuse may not seem like a big deal in friendships, but as Thom pointed out, "It doesn't matter if you're a kid, teen, or adult. Your friends are not supposed to hit you or hurt you. Ever."[2]

1. Kai Cheng Thom, "8 Signs Your Friendship Might Be Abusive," *Everyday Feminism*, March 20, 2016. everydayfeminism.com/2016/03/signs-friendship-abusive/.
2. Thom, "8 Signs Your Friendship Might Be Abusive."

- using violent behaviors as a way to bargain—for instance, by promising not to punch walls if their partner will promise not to dress a certain way
- making threats about how much worse things could be
- being severely verbally abusive

It is important to note that if someone is wondering whether their partner will escalate from verbal to physical abuse, this is enough reason to get out of the relationship. Doing mental calculations about whether there is a chance of getting physically hurt is not normal in a healthy relationship.

Rihanna, Chris Brown, and Traumatic Bonding

Many people have an unrealistic view of domestic violence because of the way it is shown in movies, TV shows, and songs as well as in the news. Pop culture sometimes portrays abuse as a sign of love or as something that is not actually a problem. For instance, the song "Kiss with a Fist" by Florence + The Machine talks about a couple who kick and punch each other and includes the line, "A kick in the teeth is good for some / A kiss with a fist is better than none."[11]

Another artist who sings about love and abuse is Rihanna, who was violently beaten by her then-boyfriend, Chris Brown, in 2009. Immediately after the incident, Rihanna left Brown and said in an interview that she chose to leave because she wanted to be a role model to young girls who were in abusive relationships. However, in 2012, Rihanna gave another interview in which she sympathized with Brown, saying that his abuse had been a mistake he made because he needed help. The couple got back together and recorded the song "Nobody's Business." The lyrics imply that domestic violence is a private matter between a couple. However, as the *Washington Post* pointed out in an article about the song, accepting domestic violence as normal sets a bad example for others in abusive relationships. The article stated that "domestic violence, the propensity of some to accept it, its causes, and its aftermath is everyone's business."[12]

Many people wondered why Rihanna went back to Brown after she had left. Tricia Bent-Goodley, a professor of social work at Howard University, said people who return to an abusive relationship often do so because of several different factors, including "cultural beliefs that physical abuse is a normal part of being in a relationship, and romanticizing what your relationship used to be versus what it actually is and whatever

The relationship between Rihanna and Chris Brown was frequently in the news. Rather than questioning why Brown hurt Rihanna, many people questioned why she got back together with him.

is actually going on internally with the individual who has been victimized."[13]

The music video for Rihanna's hit song "We Found Love" offers additional insight when Rihanna speaks at the beginning. She says, "You almost feel ashamed that someone could be that important, that without them, you feel like nothing … You feel hopeless, like nothing can save you. And when it's over and it's gone, you almost wish that you could have all that bad stuff back so that you could have the good."[14] This mindset is common among people who have been in abusive relationships because in between the abuse, the abuser is frequently loving and caring. This is one way abusers get their partner to stay so long. Bancroft explained,

The Role of Race and Culture

There is a myth, particularly in the United States, that certain cultures approve of and encourage abuse of women. These accusations are generally motivated by racism; in reality, abusers exist everywhere in the world, regardless of race or culture. However, Bancroft noted that the ways in which the abuse happens often differ depending on a person's cultural values: "Middle-class white abusers, for example, tend to have strict rules about how a woman is allowed to argue. If she talks back to him, shows anger, or doesn't shut up when she is told to, he is likely to make her pay."[1] In contrast, he wrote, men from Latin American cultures are more likely to tolerate this behavior from women but less likely to tolerate her giving attention to other men, no matter how innocent.

In the United States, where black people—especially black men—are targeted by police and are frequently victims of what some people see as unfair jail sentences, race can play a role in a woman's willingness to report her abuser. Social work professor Tricia Bent-Goodley explained,

> *While domestic violence impacts all communities, black women are further burdened with the fear of going to the police and the courts because they don't want to turn black men over to the criminal justice system. They don't want to bring shame to the community and they don't want others to think negatively about them and about black men because they have the added dimension of racism and discrimination to contend with. It can be a crippling burden no matter your economic status.*[2]

Additionally, when women of color bring an abuse case to court against a white abuser, their abuser is often protected by both white privilege and male privilege, making it harder for the woman to receive justice.

1. Lundy Bancroft, *Why Does He Do That?: Inside the Minds of Angry and Controlling Men*. New York, NY: G.P. Putnam's Sons, 2002, pp. 76-77.
2. Quoted in Michelle Bernard, "Rihanna and Chris Brown Are Proof that Domestic Violence Is Everyone's Business," *Washington Post*, February 11, 2013. www.washingtonpost.com/blogs/she-the-people/wp/2013/02/11/rihanna-and-chris-brown-are-proof-that-domestic-violence-is-everyones-business/?noredirect=on&utm_term=.90f3aae2b60e.

Life with an abuser can be a dizzying wave of exciting good times and painful periods of verbal, physical, or sexual assault. The longer the relationship lasts, the shorter and farther apart the positive periods tend to become ... After [an abusive episode], he typically acts ashamed or regretful about his cruelty and violence, at least in the early years of a relationship. Then he may enter a period when he reminds you of the man you fell in love with—charming, attentive, funny, kind. His actions have the effect of drawing you into a repetitive traumatic cycle in which you hope each time that he is finally going to change for good.[15]

This process creates a condition experts call traumatic bonding or trauma bonding. The pain of abuse traumatizes a person—it scares and upsets them so badly that they desperately need comfort and affection. When the abuser stops hurting their partner and starts being kind again, the victim gets the comfort they need, and the relief is often so strong that instead of feeling angry about the previous abuse, the partner feels grateful to their abuser for being nice. This ends up making the victim feel closer to their partner; they

Traumatic bonding causes psychological changes that make it extremely hard for someone to leave an abusive relationship.

sometimes start to falsely believe the abuse was traumatic for both partners and that it was an experience they escaped together. Because of traumatic bonding, abuse victims may see people who try to get them to leave the relationship as enemies who are just jealous of the "love" the victim and their abuser share. Traumatic bonding also makes it harder to leave an abusive partner than a nonabusive partner.

For people who have left and returned, such as Rihanna (although as of 2018, she is not in a relationship with Brown), it can be difficult for them to imagine that anyone else could love them the way their abuser seems to in the good periods. This is especially true if the abuser has been breaking down their self-esteem; many abusers will specifically tell their victims things such as, "I'm the only one who would ever want to be with you," or "No one could love you as much as I do." After hearing this enough times, the victim starts to believe it. However, this is simply a tactic abusers use to keep their partner from leaving.

Physical Abuse in the Media

The idea that people must take the bad with the good in a relationship is widespread and reinforced by the media. While this is true to a certain extent in that no relationship is perfect all the time, there is a point where a line is crossed and bad behavior becomes abusive behavior, and this line is frequently crossed in pop culture. In movies and TV shows, dysfunctional relationships—where both partners yell and throw things at each other—are often shown as being very passionate. In some cases, the relationship is clearly a bad one, but in many others, the show intends for viewers to root for the relationship.

On one end of the spectrum is the hit HBO television series *Big Little Lies*. The show's first season dealt with the topics of domestic violence and sexual assault in a very honest way, and it was praised for treating those issues as serious problems and shining a light on why many women stay in abusive relationships. Nicole Kidman won an Emmy Award in 2017 for playing Celeste Wright, a victim of domestic violence, and

SHOWING WHY WOMEN STAY

"[On *Big Little Lies*] we see the many complex reasons a victim might choose not to leave her abuser—both the genuine love she feels for her husband and the shared history and family life that binds them together, as well the complicated mix of denial, guilt, and shame that many victims feel after having their self-esteem decimated by an ongoing cycle of abuse."

—Anna Silman, writer for *The Cut*

Anna Silman, "3 Relationship Counselors On What *Big Little Lies* Tells Us About Domestic Violence," *The Cut*, March 21, 2017. www.thecut.com/2017/03/couples-counselors-on-domestic-violence-and-big-little-lies.html.

she said the following upon winning the award: "We shined a light on domestic abuse … it exists far more than we allow ourselves to know. It is filled with shame and secrecy, and by you acknowledging me with this award, it shines a light on it even more, so thank you."[16]

Unfortunately, many other television shows depict abusive relationships as "relationship goals." For example, fans of the popular teen drama *Gossip Girl* loved the characters of Blair Waldorf and Chuck Bass so much as a couple that one blogger started her criticism of them with the warning, "Do not send angry letters about this. I know that everyone loves Chuck and Blair, and to say negative things about these two amounts to sheer blasphemy. But hear me out." She went on to write, "Chuck is not a good person. We watch him attempt to rape not one, but two women … in the very first episode … He's emotionally abusive, often threatening [Blair], yelling at her, and performing violent outbursts when she doesn't perform like [he] wants."[17] In one episode, Chuck becomes angry with Blair, gets drunk, attempts to assault her, and then smashes a glass window next to her face, resulting in a cut on her cheek. The executive producer of the show, Joshua Safran, defended this scene in a comment that drew widespread criticism for the way it played directly into society's view of abusive relationships as passionate and loving:

I think it's very clear that Blair is not afraid in those moments, for herself. They have a volatile relationship, they always have, but I do not believe … that it is abuse when it's the two of them. Chuck does not try to hurt Blair. He punches the glass because he has rage, but he has never, and will never, hurt Blair. He knows it and she knows it, and I feel it's very important to know that she is not scared—if anything, she is scared for Chuck— and what he might do to himself, but she is never afraid of what he might do to her.[18]

This view—that the abused partner has more sym- pathy and fear for the abuser than for herself and that physical violence or threats between two particular people does not count as abuse because it makes the relationship passionate—is exactly how real-life abusers try to get their victims to think. Jennifer Arrow, who interviewed Safran for *E! News*, noted that although Blair did actually get hurt in this scene from the flying glass, the cut was "the most perfect, beautiful, dainty injury,"[19] which she felt was highly symbolic. Her opinion of the cut shows that she and many other viewers did not see the abuse as a serious incident. Romanticizing the actions of characters such as Chuck is dan- gerous because it makes people

Blair Waldorf and Chuck Bass's relationship was seen by many fans as romantic, even though other viewers stated that it was abusive.

more willing to endure abuse in their own relationships. This is especially true when the abusive character is shown to change over time in response to the love they feel for or are shown by their partner—something that misleads real-life abuse victims into believing they, too, can change their abuser with love. In reality, there is no way for someone to be certain that a person who becomes violent when they are angry will not turn that violence on their partner in a repeated pattern of behavior. In most cases, this is exactly what does happen. Spreading the idea that abuse is a sign of passion or can be cured with enough love leads to people being physically hurt and potentially killed by an abusive partner.

In this example, not only is Chuck physically abusive to Blair by threatening her and becoming violent around her, they are both also emotionally abusive. This type of abuse is much more commonly portrayed as "real" love than physical abuse—so much so that some people believe emotional abuse is necessary for someone to prove their love.

CHAPTER 2

Emotional Abuse

Emotional abuse—also sometimes called mental or psychological abuse—is more common than physical abuse, but it is frequently difficult to identify, even for the person who is on the receiving end of it. While some instances of emotional abuse seem fairly obvious—for instance, when a person constantly insults their partner, calling them things such as "stupid" or "ugly"—many others are so subtle that the victim is not entirely sure why they feel upset afterward. This difficulty in identifying their own feelings makes it nearly impossible to explain to someone else what they are going through, which, in turn, makes it much harder to identify abuse and seek help. For the same reason, statistics on emotional abuse are unreliable. Most people do not report instances of emotional abuse, either because they do not realize it is happening until they have left the relationship, they have been convinced by their abuser that they are overreacting to a normal situation or are to blame for the abuse, or they are too afraid or embarrassed to report what is happening to them. Because of this, it is hard for researchers to study emotionally abusive relationships. Many of the currently available statistics are old, and all of the numbers are certainly too low.

Emotional abusers use multiple tactics, and it is important to remember that the tactics they use can vary. An abuser may use many tactics but change the days on which they use them. Alternatively, they may use only one or two consistently. Multiple tactics are generally combined, and these behaviors are generally repeated. In other words, someone who makes an unreasonable demand of their partner once is likely not an abuser, especially if they apologize later and make an effort not to do it again. In contrast, someone who consistently makes unreasonable demands and refuses to stop even after being asked to is being abusive, especially if they also criticize and isolate their partner.

Emotional abuse is often difficult to identify while it is happening.

Abusers may also apologize for their actions, but they do so in a way that shows they are not sincere. Sometimes they add the word "but" to excuse themselves; for instance, they may say, "I'm sorry, but you made me lose my temper." Other times, their apology may be so over the top that their partner ends up comforting them instead. In this type of apology, the abuser may cry, say negative things such as, "I don't know why you're even with me," or repeatedly beg for forgiveness. In this way, the abuser gets their victim to tell them they are forgiven while never addressing the behavior that led to the apology in the first place. If the victim tries to address the problem later, the abuser often gets angry and accuses their partner of bringing up old issues. According to experts, an apology is useless unless it is backed up with actions such as allowing the other person time to work through their feelings of anger; listening to their partner without interrupting, blaming, or making excuses; making every attempt possible to fix the situation, such as by picking up items that were thrown; and making a clear effort not to engage in the problematic behavior anymore.

What About Men?

As with physical abuse, in heterosexual relationships, some men are emotionally abused, but it happens to women much more often. However, women are often portrayed as nagging or constantly complaining about their husbands, which some people have claimed is emotionally abusive. While this is not loving behavior, most experts agree that it is generally not abuse. The Canadian anti-domestic violence organization Springtide Resources explained why women are most often the victims of emotional abuse:

> Emotional abuse, just like any other form of abuse, is about power. Women may exhibit some of the be-haviours labeled as abuse, but it is critical to assess whether her actions give her power and make her partner fearful of her. Research has shown that being female is the single largest risk factor for being a victim of abuse in heterosexual relationships, something that is clearly reflective of women's lower status in our society.[1]

1. "Emotional Abuse of Women by Male Partners: The Facts," Springtide Resources, 2000. www.springtideresources.org/resource/emotional-abuse-women-male-partners-facts.

Isolation

Isolation is one of most recognizable signs of emotional abuse. An abuser knows that their victim's friends and family will express concern over the patterns they see in the relationship, so they try to limit the amount of time their partner can spend with loved ones. Loved ones build up a person's self-esteem and sense of worth, and someone with a high sense of worth is not likely to stay in an abusive relationship, which is why abusers focus on breaking down their partners emotionally—although they do not often realize the motivations behind their own actions. Additionally, abusers control their partners because they are possessive. They want their partner's attention focused solely on them all the time. According to Bancroft, "Because of this mind-set, an abusive man tends to perceive any relationships that his partner develops, whether with males or females, as threats to him."[20]

Abusers isolate their victims in different ways. They may tell their partner they do not approve of a particular friend group or family member—often one who is trying to convince the victim to leave the relationship—or outright forbid their partner to see other people. An abuser may also constantly check in with their partner, texting and calling them to find out where they are at all times. Some install tracking apps on their partners' phones or require them to check in on social media wherever they go. Sometimes no special software is needed; according to the British newspaper *The Guardian*, "if you know, or can guess, the password to someone's cloud account, you can follow their movements constantly via the software designed to find lost or stolen phones that comes installed on many devices."[21] However, some abusers go further and install spyware that allows them to watch their partner through their phone's camera as well as see what they type, learn who they contact, and listen to their calls.

Some people are horrified by this level of watchfulness, while others misinterpret it as a sign of love. *The Guardian* mentioned a woman who found out that her husband had been tracking her through a spyware app: "She was initially shocked, she said, but didn't see it as spying—instead interpreting [his] actions as a mark of his concern for her wellbeing."[22] However, being watched all the time contributes to isolating the victim of abuse. According to Clare Laxton, who was a public policy manager at an organization called Women's Aid,

> *They will use the information to belittle or threaten the woman … They'll say: "Why were you at this restaurant? You're cheating on me, I'm going to kill myself." It closes down that woman's space, so she won't want to go out and socialise, because she knows the abuse she'll get when she gets home isn't worth it. It's all part of controlling her as much as possible.[23]*

Many people believe it is a sign of love when someone's partner texts or calls them frequently, but when it is done as a way to constantly check up on someone's behavior and location, it is controlling and abusive.

Isolation can be relatively easy to spot, both for the victim and for their friends and family. The abused partner will generally be aware that they are no longer allowed to see certain people, and their loved ones may also notice. However, sometimes it can take time for the pattern to become clear. Many

THE PSYCHOLOGICAL IMPACT OF BEING MONITORED

"I feel like I'm some sort of crazy woman who is totally paranoid, and that's not how I normally conduct my life ... I'm a rational, sane person, but that is taken away from me, along with my freedom to be myself, and be the parent I want to be. I feel trapped."

—Isobel (name changed), a woman whose abusive estranged husband monitors her movements through her mobile devices

Quoted in Rachel Williams, "Spyware and Smartphones: How Abusive Men Track Their Partners," *The Guardian*, January 25, 2015. www.theguardian.com/lifeandstyle/2015/jan/25/spyware-smartphone-abusive-men-track-partners-domestic-violence.

people spend less time with friends and family when they first get into a relationship, even a nonabusive one, so loved ones may think this is the reason for the person's sudden distance. Additionally, "the person being abused is likely to cover for the abuser. They may be blinded by love and unaware of the isolation taking place or they could be so scared of the abuser that they choose to [lie about what is happening] due to fear."[24]

Gaslighting

In contrast to isolation, gaslighting can be incredibly hard to identify. It is "a tactic in which a person or entity, in order to gain more power, makes a victim question their reality."[25] The term comes from a 1938 play called *Gaslight* in which a woman's husband tries to make her think she is insane by doing things such as turning down the gas-powered lights in their house, which makes them dim. When she tells him the lights are dimmer than they used to be, he says she is imagining it.

Today, gaslighting can be applied to any action that makes the target question their sanity or perception of reality. For instance, an abuser may hide their partner's car keys to prevent them from leaving the

In Gaslight, *which was made into a movie in the United States in 1944, the main character begins to doubt her own perceptions of reality because her husband is lying to her. Because of the movie title, this behavior is now known as gaslighting.*

house but swear that they did not touch them and that their partner simply lost them. Later, the abuser may put the keys in another spot and allow the victim to find them, while telling the victim they must have forgotten they put the keys there. Like all abuse tactics, it is about control: It makes the victim more dependent on their abuser because they believe their own perceptions of reality cannot be trusted.

As an abuse tactic, gaslighting works very well—especially when directed at women, who are often seen in society as overly sensitive, emotional, and irrational. Over time, a person does begin to question their sanity because the abuser acts as though their victim is truly insane. Signs of gaslighting include:

- saying things that are clearly lies but denying that they are lying even when confronted with proof
- starting with small lies and working up to bigger ones
- disconnection between a person's words and actions (for instance, apologizing for an action but continuing to do it)
- accusing the victim of the same things they do themselves (for instance, a cheater may accuse their partner of cheating on them)
- telling the victim that other people agree with the abuser (for instance, "Your best friend agrees with me that you're forgetful."), even if other people have not actually made those statements
- telling the victim other people are lying to them
- telling other friends and family that the victim is acting crazy or making up cruel things the victim supposedly said behind their backs
- changing the subject suddenly during an argument
- insisting they know what their partner is thinking or feeling and refusing to believe their partner when they say it is not true
- purposely taking statements the wrong way to make their partner's argument seem ridiculous

Most people have lied on occasion in an effort to avoid the consequences of actions they regret, and sometimes people remember a situation much differently than someone else does, which may lead to an argument about what truly happened. However, gaslighting refers to a deliberate pattern of lies and denial in a specific effort to make another person doubt their view of reality. Because abusers are often able to alternate charm and abuse, they generally make the victim feel guilty

Religion and Abuse

Abuse is not an official teaching of any major religion, but a person's faith can be used against them by an abuser. Some religions say that people should not get divorced. There are also some passages in religious texts such as the Bible that encourage a wife's obedience to her husband. These ideas can be used by an abuser to convince a religious victim that God would not approve of her leaving the marriage. They may convince their partner that others in their religious community would agree, which can keep an abuse victim from seeking help from their religious friends.

Sometimes other members of a religion do agree with the idea that a marriage should be preserved at all costs. Not everyone thinks this way, but if a person seeks help from their religious leader or another member of their religious community to leave an abusive relationship and is told that God would not want them to get a divorce, it can be discouraging enough to prevent them from trying again. Chad Ashby, a Southern Baptist minister, explained why he believes Christians should not view divorce as the worst thing that could happen in a relationship. In an article for *Christianity Today*, he wrote, "The point is that all of Jesus' teachings on divorce are directed at people who are looking to justify themselves when there are no grounds for divorce … Ultimately, Christians have to be people who are concerned with saving people even more than they are with saving marriages."[1]

1. Chad Ashby, "God Hates Abuse," *Christianity Today*, May 11, 2018. www.christianitytoday.com/ct/2018/may-web-only/patterson-sbc-divorce-god-hates-abuse.html.

for believing, even temporarily, that they may have been lying to them, which makes it even harder for the victim to notice the pattern.

Gaslighting can range from mild to severe, and it often escalates over time. Abuse expert Darlene Lancer explained,

> *The person gaslighting you might act hurt and indignant or play the victim when challenged or questioned. Covert [secret] manipulation can easily turn into overt [obvious] abuse, with accusations that you're distrustful, ungrateful, unkind, overly sensitive, dishonest, stupid, insecure, crazy, or abusive. Abuse might escalate to anger and intimidation with punishment, threats, or bullying if you don't accept the false version of reality.*[26]

Threats

Abusers often use threats and blackmail to control their victims. Some threats play on the victim's compassion for and emotional connection to the abuser. For example, it is common for abusers to threaten to kill themselves if their partner leaves them. They may also make statements such as, "I'd die without you," or "You're the only one I can trust." These statements do not seem threatening on the surface, and in fact, many people misread them as romantic statements. However, they are actually designed to make the victim feel sorry for the abuser and continue to accept the abuse. It is unfair for a partner in any relationship, romantic or otherwise, to make the other person completely responsible for their partner's emotional well-being. It is impossible for one person to meet all of another person's needs, which is why people in healthy romantic relationships typically have multiple healthy friendships and family relationships, too. The idea of being another person's reason for living or their only friend is frequently used as a romantic idea in pop culture, but in reality, it places a large burden on people.

Other threats are targeted at a person's sense of self and community. Threatening to accuse a victim of crimes such as rape, child abuse, or theft makes people fear being wrongly arrested or looked down on by others. Even if the threatened accusation is not a crime, it could have unpleasant consequences.

Stalking

The legal definition of stalking varies from state to state, but generally, it describes following or harassing someone in a way that makes the victim fear for their safety or the safety of their family. Experts say that although women can be stalkers, this crime is most often committed by men.

The first thing that often comes to mind when someone says the word "stalker" is a person who is showing up in places where they know the other person will be, such as at a class the stalker does not have, outside the victim's home, or at their place of work. However, stalking can also include actions such as sending threatening notes or text messages as well as giving unwanted gifts. The casual term "Facebook stalking," which typically means checking a person's social media accounts to learn things the person posted publicly, such as if they are in a relationship, is not legally considered stalking. However, social media can be used to stalk someone, such as by sending someone threatening direct messages (DMs) or by seeing where someone has checked in to find out where they are physically so they can show up at the same place. This is called cyberstalking.

Sometimes stalking is done deliberately as a way for an abuser to control their partner. This can happen both during and after a relationship; for example, a partner who has left their abuser may be stalked as the abuser attempts to scare them into restarting the relationship. Other times, people are unaware that they have become stalkers. They believe they are showing romantic interest in someone they are not yet in a relationship with and are often convinced that if they simply have enough contact with their target, the other person will return their love. In reality, most people are afraid of their stalkers, not romantically interested in them, and stalking—in addition to being illegal—shows a lack of respect for a person's privacy. Unlike most domestic abusers, people who stalk those they do not know well generally have severe mental disorders.

For instance, if the abuser threatens to tell their victim's friends and family that the abuse victim has a substance use disorder or has been saying rude things behind their loved ones' backs, the victim may stay in the abusive relationship out of fear that their loved ones will view them differently after they hear the lie. They may fear losing their other relationships so much that they stay in the abusive one.

Blackmail is another control tactic abusers often use. Blackmail occurs when the victim does actually have a secret they do not want others to know. Unlike a threat to spread false information, blackmail is a threat to spread true information. For example, if the abuser knows their partner cheated on an exam, they may threaten to tell a school official if their partner does not do what they want.

Making Demands

In a healthy relationship, people may ask each other to do or avoid doing certain things, but they understand that the other person has the choice to say no. In an abusive relationship, one person is never given the option of "no." An abusive person may tell their partner what they are allowed to wear, who they are allowed to see, where they are allowed to go, and other similar demands. Sometimes they do this outright, with statements such as, "I don't want you wearing that dress anymore," or "You shouldn't wear makeup when we're not together." Other times, they try to make their partner feel guilty by implying that their partner would not say no if they truly loved the abuser.

Bancroft noted that abusers who try to control all aspects of their partner's life by making these demands—a type of abuser he calls the Drill Sergeant—are particularly likely to become physically violent:

> The Drill Sergeant is, unfortunately, almost sure to be physically violent sooner or later, probably beginning with threats and then eventually escalating to assault. If his partner stands up to him, such as by attempting to preserve any of her rights to freedom, his violence and threats are likely to escalate until she is hurt or terrified enough that she submits to his control. He is a risk to beat his partner up to the point of severe injury.[27]

Another way an abuser may make demands is to require their partner to do things that are unfair to ask of another person. For example, the abuser may demand that their partner always have breakfast on the table when the abuser wakes up. If the victim does not obey, even unintentionally—for instance, if they over-sleep one day—the abuser will yell at them and potentially hurt them physically.

Criticizing, Blaming, and Humiliating

Abusers use multiple tactics to make their partner feel unworthy. They will often criticize their partner about aspects of their appearance or personality, and often, their accusations are false. This includes telling the victim they are ugly, stupid, annoying, sexually promiscuous, rude, untrustworthy, or uncompassionate. They may also say things such as, "I'm the only one who could ever love you." This statement is intended to make the victim feel that they are such a deeply flawed person that the abuser is the only one in the world who could overlook those flaws. The idea of a life without love is scary to most people, so this can encourage them to stay in the relationship. However, in reality, the abuser is often making the victim see flaws where none exist.

Abusers do not only say negative things about their partner in private, they also make comments in public to humiliate their partner and make them feel as though everyone else agrees that they are worthless. However, in public, the humiliation is generally subtler. If an abuser outright called their partner ugly or stupid in public, most people would think that type of behavior was out of line. Instead, they do things such as telling stories that show their partner in a negative light and getting others to laugh at things the abuser knows are embarrassing for the victim. They may also reveal things their partner told them in confidence, such as their insecurities, embarrassing stories, or things they did wrong in the past.

When someone confronts their abuser about this behavior, the abuser may respond either by gaslighting the victim—for instance, by insisting that their partner never told them to keep certain information private, even though their partner vividly remembers having that conversation—or by blaming their partner. When the victim brings up some behavior they find upsetting, the abuser generally will not acknowledge it or apologize. Instead, they will flip the situation around, inventing reasons for why the victim "made" the abuser behave that way. By the end of the argument, the victim has often become convinced that they were actually the one in the wrong, and they may end up apologizing to their abuser for the way they behaved, even if they did nothing wrong.

ABUSE CAN BE QUIET

"What you have to understand is that my mother never raised her voice and when I confronted her about her treatment of me—her put-downs and criticisms, how she said I was the problem because I was too sensitive—that was the first thing she said: 'How can you accuse me of that when I never raised my voice, not once, to you or anyone else?' Well, abuse can be very quiet."

–Kaitlyn, abuse victim

Quoted in Peg Streep, "The Brutal Truth About 6 Types of 'Quiet' Verbal Abuse," *Psychology Today*, January 27, 2017. www.psychologytoday.com/us/blog/tech-support/201701/the-brutal-truth-about-6-types-quiet-verbal-abuse.

The Silent Treatment

Sometimes after an argument, people need to be alone for a few hours to cool off and feel better. This is normal. However, in an abusive relationship, the victim may find themselves being completely ignored for days or even weeks. This may be in response to an argument in which the victim called out the abuser's behavior, or it may be a tactic the abuser is using to punish the victim for a particular behavior, even if that behavior is not wrong or bad. For example, if the victim goes out with friends one night, the abuser may not speak to them again until they apologize for doing so. In this example, the abuser is using the silent treatment to control their partner's social group; they are teaching their partner that enjoying time with friends has negative consequences.

The silent treatment is also a way for abusers to control the communication in the relationship. They decide what will be discussed and when. If there is something they do not want to talk about—for example, their own abusive behavior—using the silent treatment can offer them a way to avoid ever taking responsibility for their actions. Typically, their partner will be the first one to give in and apologize, hoping to make the situation better.

The silent treatment involves refusing to look at, speak to, or otherwise acknowledge another person. It can be deeply hurtful, especially when it goes on for weeks.

Being ignored, especially in situations where the person was not expecting it, can have a very negative effect on a person's mental health and self-esteem. When someone refuses to acknowledge another person, it sends a message that the person being ignored does not matter. When abusers alternate between periods of silence and periods of loving attention and care, it keeps their partner off-balance, always questioning how their abuser truly feels about them. This often creates a situation where the abuse victim tries desperately to do the "right" things, believing that if they do, their partner will stop giving them the silent treatment. In reality, experts have stated that the abuser will always find something wrong with their victim's behavior to punish them for because this helps them maintain control in the relationship.

Emotional Abuse in the Media

All too often, these acts of emotional abuse are seen as loving. Many people believe it is romantic if their partner gets jealous when they talk to others, wants to know what they are doing every moment of the day, or says things such as, "You are my only reason for living." As Bancroft noted,

> A man's jealousy can be flattering. It feels great that he is wildly in love with you, that he wants you so badly. But a man can be crazy about you without being jealous. Possessiveness shows that he doesn't love you as an independent human being but rather as a guarded treasure. After a while, you will feel suffocated by his constant vigilance.[28]

According to the organization Love Is Respect, one in three young adults in the United States experiences physical, sexual, emotional, or verbal abuse from a dating partner. Part of the reason why young adults are more likely to tolerate abuse may be because of what they see being held up as "relationship goals" in the media.

POP CULTURE INFLUENCES PEOPLE

"Signs of abusive relationships, including hypercriticism, possessiveness, isolation, and violent threats can be difficult to recognize in real life situations, especially when your favorite characters experience the same things. Thus, allowing abusive relationships to flourish in fictional situations can influence teens (and everyone, really) to accept them as the norm."

—Emma Mantooth, *Odyssey* writer

Emma Mantooth, "Why Pop Culture Must Stop Glorifying Toxic Relationships," *Odyssey*, August 23, 2016. www.theodysseyonline.com/pop-culture-must-stop-glorifying-toxic-relationships.

Many popular movies, books, TV shows, and songs portray an abusive relationship as a loving one. One example is the *Twilight* series of books and movies. Although most fans saw the relationship between Edward Cullen and Bella Swan as loving and romantic, others noted that it shows many clear signs of abuse. *Wired* magazine gave several examples: "Edward controls who Bella is allowed to associate with, threatens to kill himself if anything happens to her and frequently scares her in a variety of ways such as by driving too fast or abandoning her in the woods after breaking up with her."[29] In the third installment of the series, *Eclipse*, Edward goes so far as to dismantle the engine of Bella's truck so she is unable to see her friend Jacob, whom Edward believes to be dangerous and who exhibits his own abusive behavior by forcing Bella to kiss him. Instead of being upset by this behavior, many fans saw it as romantic—a sign that Edward was willing to do anything to protect Bella from a perceived threat. The book reinforces this: Bella gets angry about her truck engine, then appears to decide her anger is unreasonable.

Similarly, the book and film series *Fifty Shades of Grey* shows an abusive relationship between the main characters,

*The way people view pop culture can have a dramatic effect on their
relationships. Many* Twilight *fans, for example, expressed
a strong desire to have a boyfriend who was just like Edward (left).*

Anastasia Steele and Christian Grey. The series was originally based on *Twilight*, so it is unsurprising that many of the same behaviors show up. While *Twilight* was mainly popular with young adults, *Fifty Shades of Grey* has become popular with those over the age of 18. Christian Grey is described as charming, rich, and handsome; he pays a lot of attention to Anastasia, and he showers her with gifts. Many people focus on these parts of his personality and ignore or excuse his abusive actions. In one example, Christian shows up at a bar Anastasia is at, just in time to rescue her from being sexually assaulted by one of her male friends. He knew she was there because he had secretly put a tracking device on her phone. As with *Twilight*, fans excused this action, believing it was justified because it saved Anastasia from danger.

Some people believe that Christian's wealth is a large part of why fans excuse or ignore his abusive actions. For instance, in another scene, Christian buys Anastasia an expensive new car and sells her old one, all without asking her. Again, this was seen as romantic by many people. This may be because people tend to identify with characters in books they enjoy. In this case, many people would enjoy receiving a surprise new car from their boyfriend or husband. This makes them see the action as romantic because they overlook the fact that when this takes place in the book, Christian and Anastasia have only known each other for a little while, and he had not asked her permission to replace her personal possessions. This action is also a sign of abuse because this type of large gift often makes people feel indebted.

Abusers sometimes use gifts or favors as a way to control their partner. An action known as "loan sharking" or "favor sharking" involves doing something nice for someone else without being asked, then later bringing it up as a way to pressure the victim into doing something in return. If the victim protests that they did not want or expect the favor or gift in the first place, the abuser will make them feel guilty for not appreciating the things they do for them. In a healthy relationship, partners do not keep score this way.

In real life as well as in the media, the line between what is abuse and what is not can get blurry. People may get caught

FAVOR SHARKING IN FICTION

"'I am going out to the front porch,' his friend said, 'and there I will walk up and down until I have thought of a story for you, even though it is very cold outside, and I have no coat. I will do this for you.'

'Please don't,' the fisherman said.

'Why are you making me feel guilty for trying to do something nice for you?' his friend said.

'I do not know how to stop hurting you,' the fisherman cried. 'I must be doing something very wrong.'"

—from "Good Fences Make Good Neighbors"
by Daniel Mallory Ortberg

Mallory Ortberg, "Good Fences Make Good Neighbors" in *The Merry Spinster: Tales of Everyday Horror.* New York, NY: Henry Holt and Company, 2018, p. 185.

up in asking themselves whether a particular action can truly, definitively be considered abuse. They may wonder whether their partner really understood what they were doing, whether it was intentional or not, and how many chances they should give someone. Additionally, some people believe a relationship is not abusive if both partners act the same way, even if their behavior is unpleasant. However, even if it is unclear whether or not a particular action fits the definition of abuse, there are some behaviors that are unhealthy in any type of relationship.

CHAPTER 3

Unhealthy Behaviors and Red Flags

Going by the definition Bancroft and other experts have for abuse, an action is abusive when it is controlling and involves some type of power imbalance between the two people in the relationship. However, even actions that do not fit this definition can be unhealthy, or toxic. According to family violence expert Dr. Steven Stosny, both men and women display toxic behaviors. However, he continued, men are more often true abusers because the tactics they use tend to work better at giving them control in the relationship.

When trying to decide if a relationship is worth staying in, a person should focus less on whether their partner fits the classic definition of "abusive" and more on how the relationship makes them feel. A relationship in which one or both of the participants are unhappy most of the time is a toxic one.

INSTINCT IS IMPORTANT

"Research indicates that a woman's intuitive sense of whether or not her partner will be violent toward her is a substantially more accurate predictor of future violence than any other warning sign."

—Lundy Bancroft, abuse expert

Lundy Bancroft, *Why Does He Do That?: Inside the Minds of Angry and Controlling Men.* New York, NY: G.P. Putnam's Sons, 2002, p. 158.

Another important thing to consider is how a person acts before anything that can be considered a "relationship" has been formed. Although abusers generally make a charming first impression, there are several warning signs—also known as red flags—people can watch out for that may help them avoid becoming involved with an abuser—although it is never a person's fault if they are unable to spot the signs until it is too late. Most importantly, people should listen to their intuition, or "gut feelings," even if they cannot think of a good reason why they feel uncomfortable.

Unhealthy Behaviors

In some relationships, both partners end up exhibiting toxic behavior. Other times, the toxic behavior comes mostly from one of the partners but does not have the same effect of exploiting power and maintaining control that abuse does. Unfortunately, these toxic behaviors are sometimes seen as normal, the same way emotional abuse often is. Some of them are specific to romantic relationships, but others can take place in any relationship, such as a friendship or family. Regardless of whether a particular behavior can be considered truly abusive, the following are unhealthy and do not contribute to a loving, respectful relationship:

- hitting or throwing things at a partner, even if they are not frightened or physically hurt by it
- testing a partner to see if they act the "right" way in certain situations; for instance, having a friend flirt with them or sending a flirty message from a fake social media account to see if they flirt back
- threatening to break up over minor things
- keeping track of favors and expecting to be paid back for each one or remembering past mistakes that someone has already apologized for and bringing them up in new arguments
- constantly making passive-aggressive statements instead of communicating openly

- blaming a partner for not doing the exact right thing at the exact right time to address the other person's emotions; for instance, getting angry if they do not offer a hug when the other person wants them to, even if this desire was never expressed out loud
- excessive and unfounded jealous behavior; for instance, demanding to see who a partner is texting or telling them they are not allowed to talk to other people of the sex they are attracted to, even if their partner has never shown signs of being unfaithful
- buying each other gifts instead of discussing relationship problems
- telling an angry, upset, or hurt partner that they have no right to feel those emotions instead of listening to their concerns

Gifts can be a nice way for couples to show appreciation for each other, but they are not a substitute for conversations about boundaries and emotions.

- sabotaging a partner (convincing them to do things that are harmful to their future, such as missing class or skipping work, in an effort to make sure their partner stays in the relationship)

Forced Teaming

People who are likely to become abusive often display a variety of behaviors that can give others clues about their true personality. One of these is something called "forced teaming," where people use words such as "we" and "us" to trick others into thinking they are part of a team. The phrase was coined by intuition expert Gavin de Becker, author of the book *The Gift of Fear*, in which he describes ways people's feelings of fear can warn them that something is not right. Forced teaming, he wrote, "is an effective way to establish premature trust because a *we're-in-the-same-boat* attitude is hard to rebuff [reject] without feeling rude."[30]

De Becker gave an example of forced teaming that a man used to get into the apartment of a woman named Kelly before sexually assaulting her. When she dropped some cans of cat food in the lobby of her apartment after coming home from the grocery store, the man picked them up and offered to help her carry her groceries upstairs. When Kelly hesitated, he said, "We better hurry … We've got a hungry cat up there."[31] It was Kelly's cat, not his, but his word choice made her feel like he was on her team, so she felt rude refusing his offer.

NICE PEOPLE ARE NOT ALWAYS GOOD

"'He was so nice' is a comment I often hear from people describing the man who, moments or months after his niceness, attacked them. We must learn and then teach our children that niceness does not equal goodness. Niceness is a decision, a strategy of social interaction; it is not a character trait."

—Gavin de Becker, author of *The Gift of Fear*

Gavin de Becker, *The Gift of Fear: Survival Signals that Protect Us from Violence*. Boston, MA: Little, Brown and Company, 1997, p. 57.

Many people find it difficult to refuse forced teaming because they do not recognize it for the manipulation tactic it is. Instead, they think someone is simply trying to be nice. Refusing a nice offer is hard for most people, which is what abusers and would-be abusers count on. They take full advantage of what is known as the social contract—the desire of most people not to appear rude.

A CALCULATED CHOICE

"Predators (I'll lump rapists, stalkers, dates who can't be broken up with and other unsavories under this term) carefully select and test their victims to look for ones who have a hard time saying no. People who can't let go choose people who can't say no."

—Jennifer Peepas (Captain Awkward), advice columnist

Jennifer Peepas, "The Art of 'No,' Continued: Saying No When You've Already Said Yes," *Captain Awkward*, March 24, 2011. captainawkward.com/2011/03/24/the-art-of-no-continued-saying-no-when-youve-already-said-yes/.

Ignoring the Word "No"

When someone does refuse a person's attempts at forced teaming, the would-be abuser generally refuses to take no for an answer. Often, they do this in a charming or flattering way. They may smile and say something such as, "Don't worry; I don't bite," or "Come on, you know you want to." If the person continues to refuse, they may start to get angry; they may call the person insulting names or say things such as, "Why are you being so rude? I was only trying to be nice."

Experts say the way a person handles being told "no" is a clue to their personality. Someone who does not accept another person's wishes is showing that they do not respect the person. However, it often takes practice to spot this tactic, and even after realizing what is happening, the power of the social contract and the wish to not seem rude can make it hard for someone to take a stand. Advice columnist Jennifer Peepas, who blogs under the name Captain Awkward, gave an example of this type of interaction:

> *Imagine you're at a party. A guy offers you a drink. You say no. He says* "Come on, one drink!" *You say* "no thanks." *Later, he brings you a soda.* "I know you said you didn't want a drink, but I was getting one for myself and you looked thirsty." *For you to refuse at this point makes you the [jerk]. He's just being nice, right? Predators use the social contract and our own good hearts and fear of being rude against us. If you drink the drink, you're teaching him that it just takes a little persistence on his part to overcome your "no." If you say* "Really, I appreciate it, but no thanks" *and put the drink down and walk away from it, you're the one who looks rude in that moment. But the fact is, you didn't ask for the drink and you don't want the drink and you don't have to drink it just to make some guy feel validated.*[32]

Someone who ignores the word "no" or actions that make it clear someone is uncomfortable is highly likely to be abusive.

Common Manipulation Tactics

Potentially abusive people often try different tactics to keep people from saying no to them or turning them down. Typecasting is the name de Becker gives to a tactic in which a predator insults

Changing Views

Some behaviors that are abusive or unhealthy are seen as romantic, especially by people who are not involved in the relationship. In many movies, for instance, a character who is in love with another character often shows how lovesick they are by doing things such as walking by the person's house, sending expensive gifts, and declaring that they will not give up until the person loves them back. Many times, this persistence is rewarded: The character's actions are often depicted as romantic, and they become the "winner" when the object of their affection chooses them. However, in reality, this kind of persistence often scares people, especially when it comes from someone they know little or nothing about.

Society's view of this type of behavior seems to be shifting from romantic to unsettling; however, the media has been slower to change. In 2017, a British man named Luke Howard who had been dumped by his girlfriend of four months brought a piano to a public place and vowed not to stop playing until she took him back. He also set up Facebook and Instagram pages to bring attention to his cause. Many news outlets reported the story as romantic and sad, expressing hope that Howard would achieve his goal. However, across the internet, many people made posts criticizing the man for his action, calling it "emotional blackmail"—a way to make the woman feel guilty for her own actions with the hope of getting her to restart the relationship. One Twitter user summed up the situation by saying, "Men, women are allowed to leave you. You are not entitled to a girlfriend. Media, stop romanticising controlling, stalker behaviour."[1] Others noted that Howard's "romantic" gesture was actually a red flag for future abusive behavior, since it showed a lack of respect for his ex-girlfriend's feelings, a sense of entitlement, and an attempt to control his ex-girlfriend through social pressure. Howard denied the claims, stating that he had only wanted to make sure his ex-girlfriend was aware of how much he loved her. He stopped playing when he was physically assaulted.

1. Quoted in Gianluca Mezzofiore, "Man Who Played Piano Non-stop After Break-up Triggers Debate on Romaticizing Harrassment," Mashable, September 13, 2017. mashable.com/2017/09/13/luke-howard-piano-backlash/#c6wEIKbMfkqT

someone in an effort to get them to prove the insult wrong. He wrote, "'You're probably too snobbish to talk to the likes of me,' a man might say, and the woman will cast off the mantle of 'snob' by talking to him."[33] This tactic is sometimes called "negging." Negging can also take the slightly different form of insulting and complimenting a girl at the same time, which is also known as giving someone a backhanded compliment. For instance, a man may point out something a woman is likely to be embarrassed about, such as her weight or appearance, and say he thinks it is cute. The goal is to make a woman grateful for the attention.

The term "negging" was popularized by pickup artists (PUAs). PUAs are men who believe that with the right tactics and scripts, they can convince women to be with them. Many are attracted to the PUA community by the mistaken belief that women only want to date rude men and will not give some men a chance if they are too nice. Others are lured in by the community's promises of increased confidence and guaranteed success with women, only to find out later that many of the tactics they learn are manipulative and abusive. According to Nathan Thompson, a former PUA, "their techniques are unethical. Manipulating people

When a PUA gets into a relationship with a woman, he often looks for other partners and refuses to pay attention to his girlfriend when they are together.

for your own selfish ends is enshrined in PUA culture."[34] Thompson continued, "Some PUAs believe that all women are subconsciously trying to entrap them in long-term relationships ... Tactics to avoid [this] involve refusing intimacy ... and freezing-out partners while you focus on seducing other women (called 'nexting'). This is the sad heart of the culture."[35]

The PUA community encourages this type of emotional abuse because PUAs view women as objects, or as Thompson put it, "a code to be broken instead of human beings."[36] PUAs, like all abusers, often come across as charming at first. They then use a variety of manipulation tactics to break down a woman's self-confidence and establish an immediate connection without her realizing what is happening. The PUA's goal is to make her feel as though his attention is a gift or favor to her, which is often how other abusers work as well. Some of these manipulative tactics include:

- False Time Constraint (FTC), in which the man pretends he only has a few seconds to chat. According to the magazine *Coveteur*, "Most [PUAs] suggest using some sort of FTC *while* you sit down at a girl's table, thus making them less aware of the fact that you are physically invading their space."[37]
- kino, which involves lightly touching the person's arms, hands, hair, or other body parts for a few seconds at a time to create a false sense of intimacy with a stranger. One PUA website recommended, "Don't assume she doesn't like being touched, just keep touching until she pulls away or says something."[38] This lack of respect for a woman's physical boundaries and personal space is another sign that the person is a potential abuser.
- insulting a woman's friends to make her feel more special and easier to manipulate or to stop her friends from pointing out the manipulation

These actions may make a woman feel uncomfortable without truly knowing why, and trying to explain something small but unwanted, such as "He touched my hand for a few seconds," may make others feel that she is being unreasonable. However, feeling uncomfortable, no matter why, is reason enough to avoid getting involved with the person who is making them feel that way.

Looking for Reasons

The social contract is not generally a bad thing. In most cases, it helps keep society running smoothly. This is why many people are hesitant to break it even when someone else has already pushed past its boundaries. The social contract is often reinforced by friends, family, and even strangers, especially when it comes to dating and friendships.

Most people want to know the reasons behind a person's feelings and actions, and they may discount the person's feelings if they believe their reason is not good enough. If someone says they simply "have a bad feeling" about a person, whether it is a potential romantic partner or a potential friend, they are often told to give the person a chance and not be so judgmental. Even if they are able to give a reason, they may be told that it is not a good enough explanation. However, listening to intuition is important, and no one owes anyone else the "right" reason for discontinuing contact with someone who makes them uncomfortable or upset. As blogger Jennifer Peepas (Captain Awkward) noted in one of her advice letters, "You don't have to be friends or get emotionally closer to someone you don't like. You don't have to make a convincing case for why you don't like them or hear their case out in full. They don't have to be on board with your decision not to be friends. You have done your part by being a basic amount of polite and cordial."[1] This applies both to the person in question and to any other friends or family members who ask for justification of someone's feelings.

1. Jennifer Peepas, "Consent Basics: It Takes Two to Decide to Be Friends and Only One to Say 'Nope!'," *Captain Awkward*, March 23, 2015. captainawkward. com/2015/03/23/681-it-takes-two-to-decide-to-be-friends-and-only-one-to-say-nope/.

Getting Serious Too Quickly

Sometimes the pace of a relationship makes people feel uncomfortable for reasons they cannot quite explain; they may feel silly trying to tell someone, "He texts me a lot," or "He always wants to spend time with me." In today's society, these actions are often seen as desirable, so it can be difficult for the person to explain even to themselves why they feel uncomfortable with how intense a new relationship is becoming.

Being in love feels good, so it can be hard for someone to notice when the relationship is moving too fast. Someone in a new relationship should be concerned if their partner suggests making big, sudden changes, such as getting married or moving in together.

This behavior could also act in the exact opposite way: It could draw the victim in before they are aware anything is wrong. This is especially true if the abuser is someone the victim really likes. Having someone pay close attention to them, seek out their company, and give compliments and gifts can be thrilling and make the person feel special. There is nothing wrong with showing appreciation for someone at the beginning of a relationship, but it is important to be wary if the other person gives gifts that are expensive early on in the relationship or says things such as, "I want to spend my life with you," or, "I can't imagine living without you," within only a few weeks of knowing each other. Bancroft warned,

> But watch out if he jumps too soon into planning your future together without taking enough time to get to know you and grow close, because it can mean that he's trying to wrap you up tightly into a package that he can own. Take steps to slow things down a little. If he won't respect your wishes in this regard, there is probably trouble ahead.[39]

TRUST YOURSELF

"If you feel like an action is wrong, don't do it—no matter what. If someone you like hits you or snoops in your email, you shouldn't do it in return. Your friends might tell you 'put your woman in line, she shouldn't do that, and you should take control' … Ignore them and be your own man."

—Eric Metcalf, medical professional

Eric Metcalf, MPH, "Are You in an Abusive Relationship?," WebMD, August 8, 2011. teens.webmd.com/boys/features/abusive-relationship-and-teens#3.

People may be nervous to slow things down out of fear that they will lose the other person, but someone who truly respects their partner's wishes and boundaries will listen to them.

"Not Like Other Girls"

Abusers often have a negative attitude, especially toward others. In their minds, nothing is ever their fault, so they frequently blame others and never admit their own faults. Someone who consistently says rude things about their ex-partners, such as calling them "crazy" or saying that they falsely accused the person of being abusive, is generally not telling the whole truth. Partners of heterosexual males should be extra cautious if he says demeaning things about women in general, especially if he follows it up with compliments such as, "You're not like other girls." Bancroft noted, "You will be tempted to work doubly hard to prove that you aren't like those other women, and one foot will already be in the trap. It won't be long before he is telling you that you are 'just like the rest of them.'"[40]

This negative attitude toward women often extends to gender roles. Many people have strict ideas about what women should and should not do, and people who hold these views often say and do sexist things. It can be difficult to meet someone who does not have these views, which makes many women feel tempted to settle for a level of sexism they feel is tolerable. However, men who believe in equality and respect for women exist, and it is worth waiting for them.

Some men believe there are certain things a woman is required to do in a relationship, such as cook dinner every night. Some use abuse tactics to make sure women conform to these gender roles.

Another attitude that is problematic is attraction to people who are vulnerable, or defenseless, in some way. Young women are at risk for being taken advantage of by older men, especially if they have no other relationship to compare it to. Bancroft explained,

> *Why, for example, does a twenty-two-year-old man pursue a sixteen-year-old adolescent? ... They are at completely different*

developmental points in life with a dramatic imbalance in their levels of knowledge and experience. He is attracted to power and seeks a partner who will look up to him with awe and allow him to lead her. Of course, he usually tells her the exact opposite, insisting that he wants to be with her because of how unusually mature and sophisticated she is for her age.[41]

Studies have shown that when teenage girls become pregnant, the father is often older, proving that this type of unbalanced relationship is not uncommon. Additionally, while parents in the past had fears about people on the internet lying about their identity in order to assault young women, researchers now know that the majority of internet predators are older men who are honest about their age. They get close to their target through a process known as grooming. This involves gaining the victim's trust and then manipulating them with compliments, gifts, and statements designed to make the victim feel important, such as, "You're the only one I can talk to about this." Through grooming, the predator makes the target believe they are in a romantic relationship. If this "relationship" lasts any length of time, it is generally full of abusive tactics.

Getting out of an abusive or toxic relationship can be difficult; it requires strength, courage, and support from loved ones or a professional. Fortunately, it can be done, and many people have escaped abusive relationships and gone on to find healthier, more fulfilling ones.

CHAPTER 4

Dealing with Abuse

It can take a long time for someone to realize they are in an abusive relationship, and after the truth becomes undeniable, it can take even longer for the person to be able to leave their abuser. Leaving can be dangerous, especially if the abuse is physical. It can also be difficult because by this time, the abuser often has isolated the victim from their friends and family, so they may not have a strong network of support to give them encouragement and assistance. Fortunately, there are organizations abuse victims can turn to for help.

Communication and Respect Are Key

It can be difficult for someone to tell whether a friend, partner, or family member is being abusive. Everyone does things sometimes that are hurtful to others, but the key is to notice whether the behaviors are part of a pattern—and patterns can be hard to spot when someone is in the middle of them. They may tell themselves, "It was just one time," forgetting about other times when the same thing happened. They may also think or be told by others, "All relationships have problems," "You must have done something to upset him," "You're not perfect either," or "If he apologized, you need to accept it and move on."

It is true that no one is perfect and that sometimes the only thing a person can do about their behavior is apologize and move forward. However, it is important to note that some behaviors can be overlooked or worked through for the sake of the relationship, while others should not be tolerated.

The Black Dot: An Urban Legend

Rumors are often circulated on social media long after they have been proven false. In some cases, this can be harmful. One example is the Black Dot Campaign, which tried to promote a black dot drawn in the center of a person's palm as a universal sign of abuse to alert others even if the abuser was nearby. This was quickly picked up and reposted on social media websites. However, the website Snopes, which investigates myths online, pointed out some problems with the campaign:

> The black dot campaign is merely one person's idea for helping victims of domestic violence; it is not an officially-sanctioned program, and it is not taught to police officers, doctors, counselors, or anyone else who may be able to help someone in an abusive relationship. While victims of domestic violence can certainly draw a black dot on their palms, they should not rely on that symbol's bringing anyone to their aid.[1]

Experts have said the campaign, while well-meaning, is dangerous. Most people who might know what it means are not trained to step in and help an abuse victim, and any abuser with internet access might learn about it and know why their partner has a dot on their hand. The campaign later clarified that it was only meant to help people in abusive relationships start conversations about the abuse with their loved ones. Dina Polkinghorne, the executive director of the domestic violence prevention group Project Sanctuary, suggested that victims could talk to their loved ones when the abuser is not around instead of relying on them to notice and comment on the black dot.

1. Dan Evon, "The Black Dot Campaign," Snopes, last updated November 1, 2016. www.snopes.com/fact-check/black-dot-campaign.

Behaviors such as forgetting to wash the dishes or rescheduling plans frequently may be annoying, but they are generally things that can be discussed. However, if one person dismisses the other's concerns and refuses to stop doing things even after they know it upsets their partner, this is a sign that something more serious is wrong with the relationship.

In a healthy relationship, couples feel able to talk to each other about their problems so they can reach a solution that makes both people happy.

Identifying the Signs

Rather than analyzing their partner's behavior to prove whether it is truly worth ending the relationship over, people may find it easier to examine their own feelings and behavior. Some signs that a person is in an abusive relationship include:

- They are scared to do or say anything that might upset their partner.
- They stop voicing disagreement with their partner because it is easier to stay quiet and just do what their partner wants.
- They frequently question their own emotions and perceptions of reality.
- They spend time with their partner because they feel required to, not because they want to.
- They often feel hurt by things their partner says, but when they bring it up, they are told they are "too sensitive" or "have no sense of humor."

- They apologize even when they have done nothing wrong.
- They feel unreasonable because they keep asking their partner to stop doing the same thing and their partner keeps repeating the behavior, with or without apology.
- They feel sorry for their partner even though their partner is the one hurting them.
- They feel like their boundaries and requests are being ignored.
- They are constantly thinking about how to fix the relationship rather than enjoying being in it.
- They feel like all the problems in the relationship are their fault.

Many of these signs may make a person feel as though there is something wrong with them rather than their partner, especially when the situations seem unimportant or their partner tries to pretend they are doing something nice. For example, if a woman tells her boyfriend she does not want to go out on a certain night and her boyfriend later surprises her with movie tickets for that evening, she will likely feel ungrateful if she reminds him she wanted to stay in. If she does bring it up, her boyfriend may act hurt that she does not appreciate his gift. This is a combination of several red flags: ignoring a boundary by not respecting the woman's wish to stay home on a specific evening, ignoring the word "no," and changing plans with an unwelcome surprise. Author Peg Streep explained,

> While overt control—insisting they get their own way, asserting veto power over plans, making constant demands without discussion—is easy to spot, what Dr. Craig Malkin calls "stealth control," a behavior he identifies with narcissists, is much more insidious [subtle in a bad way]. Stealth control includes changing up plans you've already made—eating at a French bistro, going to see friends—or revising joint decisions under the guise of "surprising" you with something better than the original. Of course, surprise isn't the motive; controlling you is, without ever making a demand. Alas, you're so flattered by his caring that you utterly

miss the point. In time, it becomes a pattern and your own wants and needs will fall by the wayside.[42]

Many people appreciate surprises from loved ones, but if the surprise always cancels out the person's original wishes, they may start to feel frustrated but too guilty to complain about it—especially if friends say things such as, "I wish my boyfriend was that romantic!"

#ThatsNotLove

The #ThatsNotLove campaign was started by the healthy relationship advocacy organization One Love to help people recognize the difference between loving behavior and controlling behavior, which can be especially confusing in the era of social media. People often post happy pictures of themselves when they are in a relationship, even when they are not actually happy behind the scenes. Seeing pictures of other "happy" couples can sometimes influence people to stay in an unhealthy relationship, hoping it will turn into what those around them appear to have.

#ThatsNotLove explores "the gray areas between love and control"[1] through videos that demonstrate unhealthy behaviors. Interactive materials can be downloaded or requested from the website to help people start discussions about this issue. They include discussion guides, bookmarks that can be placed in library books to warn other readers that the book promotes unhealthy relationship behaviors, and stickers people can write healthy behaviors on and stick in a public place where others can see.

1. "#ThatsNotLove," One Love, accessed on June 21, 2018. www.joinonelove.org/act/thats-not-love.

Reaching Out

Even after someone realizes they are in an abusive relationship, it can take time for them to leave. Getting out of an abusive relationship requires planning because an abuser is not likely to be okay with breaking up. Working with a trusted friend, parent, counselor, or trained advocate can help someone make a plan to stay safe, especially if their abuser is physically violent. They must be able to know where they can stay, how they can protect themselves, how they can protect any children they might have, how much money they will need, and more. This is an overwhelming amount of planning, especially for someone who has been taught by their abuser to believe they are incapable of doing anything on their own. Reaching out for help can reduce the burden of figuring out a plan and give the victim a source of moral support—a person who can reassure them that the abuse was never their fault and that they are smart enough and capable enough to leave their abuser.

Leaving an abusive relationship often requires careful planning.

Reaching out to others for help makes a big difference in an abuse victim's life. Telling a trusted friend—or an adult if the victim is under 18—is one of the first steps they can take. They may feel embarrassed or believe no one will understand, but people who care about them will realize it is the abuser who is at fault, not them.

Friendships are very important to someone who is in an abusive relationship. A friend can do a lot to help someone, including helping the victim recognize the abuse for what it is and create safety plans to get out, reminding the victim that they are strong and worthwhile, listening without judgment as the victim tries to work through their feelings about the relationship, and encouraging the victim to get help from an adult or professional organization. However, it is important for everyone involved to remember that ultimately, the person who needs to act is the victim. Domestic violence expert Barrie Levy gave this advice for friends who are trying to support an abuse victim:

> If you become frightened or frustrated, get support from friends and family members or other adults. Educate yourself about dating violence. You can't rescue your friend. You can't neglect your own life to take care of her or him. But with support for yourself, you can calmly hang in there and support your friend as she or he goes through the ups and downs of dealing with the violence [or psychological abuse].[43]

Leaving an abusive relationship can be especially difficult for someone who goes to the same school as their abuser. They may be too afraid to break up due to social pressure or the likelihood that they will continue to see their abuser every

SURVIVORS ARE STRONG

"You have a lot of strength. Remember the times you have been strong in dealing with being abused:

- Remember the times you said something or did something that kept you from being hurt worse.
- Remember the times you told someone about it.
- Remember the ways you have avoided the violence.
- Remember how you have kept going when you have felt so much pain and fear.

When you think about how you have survived the emotional pain and the physical injuries, are you surprised to realize how strong you are? You can use your strength to plan for your safety and freedom from violence."

-Barrie Levy, domestic and sexual violence expert

Barrie Levy, *In Love and in Danger: A Teen's Guide to Breaking Free of Abusive Relationships.* Berkeley, CA: Seal Press, 2006, pp. 84-85.

day. This makes reaching out especially important. Teachers and friends who are aware of the situation may be able to help; for example, the victim may get special permission to change their schedule in a way that makes it easier to avoid running into their abuser during the day, and friends may be able to prevent the abuser from cornering their former victim in an isolated spot.

If someone is too nervous or embarrassed to reach out to people they know or if they have been too isolated by their abuser to believe they can get help from loved ones, calling a hotline can be a good first step. The trained listeners on the other end of the phone can give advice on the person's individual situation and offer encouragement to help the person take the next step in ending the relationship. Hotlines can also help someone figure out how to request a domestic violence advocate who can come to court or the hospital with them. These advocates can offer advice and moral support as they make sure the victim is aware of all their rights.

THE IMPORTANCE OF GETTING OUT

"[I finally attended school in a different city.] Away from our abusive fights, I was able to build my self-reliance in small ways. I learned to have fun without Mike, to make decisions ... and to [be okay without] seeing him every day."

-Marge, teenage abuse survivor

Quoted in Barrie Levy, *In Love and in Danger: A Teen's Guide to Breaking Free of Abusive Relationships.* Berkeley, CA: Seal Press, 2006, pp. 83-84.

Involving the Police

In some cases, abuse victims need more help than they can get from friends, family, or even professional advocates. They need police intervention. Calling the police on a violent abuser can feel like a scary and unnecessary step. Abuse victims may feel pressured by others not to "ruin his life" by getting the abuser arrested. However, sometimes calling the police is necessary for the victim's protection. Marian Betancourt, the author of *What to Do When Love Turns Violent*, offered some reasons for why an abuse victim should not feel bad about calling the police on their partner:

- *Assault is a crime in all fifty states. If you were assaulted by a stranger on the street, you would expect an arrest.*

- *Abusive men get violent because they get away with it, and they get what they want. It is time they learned some other way.*

- *If a man is abusive and there are no serious consequences for his use of violence, his violent behavior is reinforced.*

- *The courts can place controls on a violent man that friends and family members cannot. They can send him to jail, levy heavy fines, restrict his bail, serve protective orders, and send him to a batterer's counseling program.*[44]

Betancourt noted that it is important for the victim to try to speak to the police in a room away from their abuser, as the abuser will likely try to remain calm and collected so the

Sometimes abuse victims call the police while the abuse is happening, then feel too scared or guilty to press charges when the police arrive. Other times, the abuser successfully convinces the police that the victim was lying. As a result, abusers are not always arrested even though they have committed a crime.

Abuse and Mass Shootings: A Wider Issue

While it is worth calling the police on a violent abuser simply for the sake of the victim's own safety, it can also have a larger benefit. Gun violence in the United States is on the rise, and recent studies have shown that domestic violence is often an indicator that a person will shoot someone besides their original victim. National Public Radio (NPR) reported that as many as 50 percent of American mass shootings were committed by someone who was abusive to their partner or family members. Additionally, a gun control group called Everytown for Gun Safety "studied all of the mass shootings that took place in the US between 2009 and 2015, and found that 57 percent of the shootings were directed at or involved members of the perpetrator's family."[1] Other research has shown that someone is more likely to be shot by their partner than by a stranger.

One example of a reported abuser who went on to commit a deadly act of gun violence is Nicolas Cruz, who killed 17 people in a mass shooting at Marjory Stoneman Douglas High School in Florida on February 14, 2018. He was reported by classmates to have been abusive to his ex-girlfriend and had fought with her new boyfriend. His violent behavior caused at least three students to report him to school officials before the date of the shooting.

The pattern of domestic abuse and gun violence has become so undeniable that it has led some states to change their laws. In 2018, Oregon passed a law to close the "boyfriend loophole" in its gun control policy. The new law "would allow police in Oregon to confiscate guns from people who stalk or abuse a partner even if they are not married to or living with the victim and do not share a child in common with the victim."[2]

Reporting abuse can potentially help police keep an eye on someone who might become violent toward a larger number of people. However, many victims do not feel safely able to report their abuser. It is never an abuse victim's fault if their abuser goes on to be violent to others.

1. Constance Grady, "Johnny Depp's Domestic Abuse Allegations Deserve as Much Attention as His Assassination Joke," Vox, June 23, 2017. www.vox.com/culture/2017/6/23/15861794/johnny-depp-assassination-joke-domestic-abuse-amber-heard.
2. "Students at the Forefront: 'Boyfriend Loophole' Closed with New Gun Law in Oregon," Break the Cycle, accessed on June 17, 2018. www.breakthecycle.org/blog/students-forefront-%E2%80%9Cboyfriend-loophole%E2%80%9D-closed-new-gun-law-oregon.

victim appears to be the one who is out of control. They may also claim that the victim is the one who attacked first or deny attacking at all if the victim's injuries are not obvious.

Whenever possible, the abuse victim should document the abuse. This means taking pictures of their injuries and any damage around them, such as shattered glass or broken objects in the home. They should also note the dates these incidents took place. This provides proof of the abuse that can be shown in court. However, a good lawyer can help figure out ways to make a strong case even if this evidence is not available.

An abuse victim may also be able to get a restraining order, although this requires help from an adult if the victim is under 18 years old. This is a court order that forbids the abuser from coming near their former victim. However, it is important to remember that sometimes abusers violate these restraining orders, so it is also a good idea for abuse victims to take other protective measures, such as learning self-defense and keeping their doors locked when they are home. If the abuser does break the restraining order, the police can be called, and the abuser can be arrested.

Domestic Violence and the Law

In 1994, the Violence Against Women Act (VAWA) was signed into law by President Bill Clinton. It focused on creating a better understanding of rape and domestic violence as serious crimes and on preventing violence by giving grants, or government funding, to shelters, rape prevention programs, and community education about domestic violence. It also classified violence against women that is committed because they are women as a hate crime, allowing women to sue their attacker in federal court. This part of the law was called the civil rights remedy. Women's groups were especially happy with VAWA because they had been telling the federal government for years that individual states were not doing enough to address domestic abuse. However, others opposed the law because they believed it was unnecessary to create laws based on gender, and the U.S. Supreme Court eventually declared the civil rights remedy unconstitutional.

VAWA was reauthorized in 2000 and again in 2013, drawing more criticism from people who were unhappy about the fact that the 2013 reauthorization also expanded the law to protect Native Americans, same-sex couples, and victims of sex trafficking. Others supported these additions, and many say the law has been an overall success. The website Legal Momentum stated,

> Despite elimination of the civil rights remedy, VAWA and its subsequent [following] reauthorizations have vastly improved services for victims of sexual and domestic violence and stalking, as well as education and training about violence against women for victim advocates, health professionals, law enforcement, prosecutors and judges.[45]

This law only protects American citizens, so undocumented immigrants who are dealing with domestic violence often do not call the police for fear that they will be deported. However, VAWA offers a path to citizenship for undocumented immigrants who are married to U.S. citizens and have been victims of domestic abuse.

Seeking Asylum for Domestic Violence

In the past, people who experienced domestic abuse in their home country and tried to escape it by coming to the United States could apply for asylum. However, in June 2018, Attorney General Jeff Sessions announced that the government would stop providing asylum to victims of gang violence and domestic violence. "Asylum" describes political protection for certain immigrants who are fleeing danger in their home countries. While refugees are people who apply to live in the United States before they leave their home country, people seeking asylum do so afterward. They come to the country before getting the proper permission, but once officials determine that they meet the criteria for asylum, they can begin applying for refugee status.

Every year, thousands of people— mainly women—seek asylum in the United States to get away from domestic violence and gang violence in their home countries.

After Sessions said that victims of gang violence and domestic violence no longer qualified for asylum, many women who came to the United States to escape these kinds of violence were considered to have committed a crime. Instead of being helped, they were arrested and detained indefinitely or deported. Sessions received criticism for his decision from civil rights groups because he has called domestic violence a "private crime," which, according to experts, is not a legal term. Some people, such as Mara Verheyden-Hilliard of the Partnership for Civil Justice Fund, have accused Sessions of returning to the outdated belief that domestic violence is a private matter between a couple. This belief, Verheyden-Hilliard and others say, places thousands of women in danger both in and out of the United States.

Difficult but Not Impossible

Although getting out of an abusive relationship is difficult, it is not impossible; many people have managed it and gone on to live healthier, happier lives. However, abuse leaves scars—some of them physical, some of them psychological. After an abusive relationship has ended, a period of healing is necessary.

Recovering from Abuse

Abuse changes a person's behavior and often makes them feel as though they do not deserve to have a healthy relationship—although nothing could be further from the truth. Survivors of domestic violence and other forms of abuse frequently develop mental illnesses such as depression, anxiety, post-traumatic stress disorder (PTSD), and complex post-traumatic stress disorder (C-PTSD). The healing process often involves dealing with these disorders and other effects of the abuse through therapy.

Abuse and Mental Disorders

An anxiety disorder is diagnosed when a person has a fear of nonthreatening events that is so strong it interferes with their ability to live normally. Some anxiety disorders, such as generalized anxiety disorder, occur seemingly without cause. Experts' best guess is that they involve an imbalance in brain chemicals that may be caused by a combination of genetics and environmental factors. Someone who was already likely to develop an anxiety disorder may end up developing one as a result of abuse.

In contrast to anxiety, PTSD is disproportionate fear that has a specific cause: exposure to a traumatic event, such as an episode of domestic violence. Previously, PTSD was considered a type of anxiety disorder, but the fifth edition of the *Diagnostic and Statistical Manual of Mental Disorders (DSM-5)* moved it to a category called Trauma- and Stressor-Related Disorders. People who have PTSD tend to relive the traumatic event through flashbacks, nightmares,

Can Abusers Change?

Many abuse victims stay with their abuser for a long time in the hope that the abuse will stop. Experts such as Bancroft say that abusers can change, but they have to truly want to and be dedicated to putting in the effort to do so. Many do not want to do this because it involves facing facts that go against things they have been taught since they were young. Messages from family members, friends, TV shows, movies, music, jokes, and other sources are all involved in forming an abuser's impression that they are better than the people around them and are entitled to anything they want. For this reason, Bancroft wrote, "the majority of abusive men do not make deep and lasting changes even in a high-quality abuser program."[1]

Some abusers do change by putting in hard work, and it is often an ongoing, lifelong process. However, abusers frequently promise to change without any intention of doing so. A promise that is not followed through with action by joining a counseling program is simply another way for an abuser to control their partner and keep them from leaving. Joining a counseling group is crucial to changing abusive patterns. Experts such as Bancroft and Levy say it cannot be done individually because someone needs to hold the abuser accountable for their behavior; the abuser often has trouble recognizing when their actions are problematic. If drugs and alcohol are contributing to the problem, joining a separate support group for that issue is also important. Abuse victims who are able to leave should not wait around to see if their abuser follows through on their promises.

The sooner people recognize and address their unhealthy behaviors, the better their chance of avoiding falling into the trap of becoming an abusive partner. Levy wrote, "Confronting your violence means changing your attitudes toward women in general, and toward victims, and developing respect for them. It means changing your attitudes about violence, until you believe that it is not acceptable."[2] Acknowledging problematic behavior is the first step to changing it.

1. Lundy Bancroft, *Why Does He Do That?: Inside the Minds of Angry and Controlling Men.* New York, NY: G.P. Putnam's Sons, 2002, p. 335.
2. Barrie Levy, *In Love and in Danger: A Teen's Guide to Breaking Free of Abusive Relationships.* Berkeley, CA: Seal Press, 2006, p. 100.

*PTSD often causes nightmares, which can make
it hard for someone to sleep at night.*

and intrusive thoughts, which are involuntary and unwelcome thoughts. These are often triggered by reminders of the event, so something that seems harmless to most people may greatly upset someone with PTSD. For instance, if a woman's abuser often told her he loved her as he was beating her, the woman may be triggered when others say that they love her. People with PTSD also experience negative thoughts and emotions, such as self-blame for the traumatic event, overly negative thoughts about the world (for instance, believing they will never have a partner who is not abusive), and difficulty experiencing positive emotions such as happiness and excitement. They often feel shame for having been abused, believing it was their fault for allowing the abuse to continue. They tend to live in a state of hypervigilance, which means constantly being on the lookout for threats even when the immediate danger has passed. They may startle easily and have difficulty sleeping, relaxing, and concentrating on tasks.

C-PTSD is similar to PTSD, but it is caused by repeated or long-term trauma, such as an extended abusive relationship. However, there is no specific time length for the cause of either PTSD or C-PTSD. In addition to the symptoms of PTSD, symptoms of C-PTSD include problems with:

- **Emotional Regulation.** *May include persistent sadness, suicidal thoughts, explosive anger, or inhibited [suppressed] anger.*

- **Consciousness.** *Includes forgetting traumatic events, reliving traumatic events, or having episodes in which one feels detached from one's mental processes or body (dissociation).*

- **Self-Perception.** *May include helplessness, shame, guilt, stigma, and a sense of being completely different from other human beings.*

- **Distorted Perceptions of the Perpetrator.** *Examples include attributing total power to the perpetrator, becoming preoccupied with the relationship to the perpetrator, or preoccupied with revenge.*

- **Relations with Others.** *Examples include isolation, distrust, or a repeated search for a rescuer.*

- **One's System of Meanings.** *May include a loss of sustaining faith or a sense of hopelessness and despair.*[46]

Depression is also often seen in abuse victims. Symptoms of depression include thoughts of worthlessness, hopelessness, despair, withdrawal from friends and family, and loss of interest in activities the person normally enjoys.

ADVICE FROM A FORMER ABUSER

"Leave and find someone else. You don't need someone who's hitting you all the time."

—Paul, age 18

Quoted in Barrie Levy, *In Love and in Danger: A Teen's Guide to Breaking Free of Abusive Relationships.* Berkeley, CA: Seal Press, 2006, p. 93.

People with any of these mental disorders often turn to drugs or alcohol as a way to make themselves feel better. However, abusing these substances causes more problems than it solves. It is an expensive habit to maintain, it causes performance at work and school to suffer, it can lead to a potentially deadly addiction, and if the substance is illegal, it can lead to jail time.

Treating Disorders

Therapy is one of the most important steps in treating the mental disorders that can arise from abuse. Several different types of therapy are available, and the most effective one will depend on the symptoms the individual has developed. Some types of therapy available for victims of abuse include:

- cognitive behavioral therapy (CBT), which helps patients identify and change negative thought patterns
- prolonged exposure (PE) therapy, which helps PTSD victims face their trauma until the memory of it no longer affects them
- eye movement desensitization and reprocessing (EMDR), which involves moving the eyes in a specific pattern while remembering the trauma to decrease the negative emotions surrounding the traumatic event
- stress inoculation training (SIT), which teaches patients how to relax their muscles and control their breathing during times of stress to help diminish the symptoms of hypervigilance and the startle response
- cognitive processing therapy (CPT), which is often described as a combination of CBT and PE

While all of these types of therapy are supported by research, each individual will experience different results. One person may find that CPT works well for them and that EMDR is not helpful at all, while another person may experience the exact opposite. It often takes some trial and error for people to find the therapist and the type of therapy that works best with their individual needs.

EMDR is a type of therapy where the patient follows an object, such as a pencil or their therapist's finger, with their eyes while remembering their trauma. Some people believe it works better for PTSD than other types of therapy, while others believe more conventional methods such as CBT work better.

People who are living with mental disorders after leaving an abusive relationship sometimes find that combining medication with therapy is the best way for them to control their symptoms. Some people do not find medications such as antidepressants helpful, but others do. People may feel uncomfortable taking medication because of society's stigma, or negative view, around this practice. Abuse victims in particular may be told that they do not need medication. Mary Emily O'Hara, a sexual assault survivor who developed PTSD, described why she initially resisted taking antidepressants: "There was nothing wrong with *me*, I thought—there was something wrong with what had happened to me. If I kept fighting, I would eventually cross the line into normalcy. Why should I have to alter my brain chemistry after everything I already suffered?"[47]

However, many health experts as well as celebrities have worked hard in recent years to change this stigma. Actress Kristen Bell has been particularly outspoken about the fact that anxiety and depression are not causes for shame, even if someone needs medication to control them. She said, "If you do decide to go on a prescription to help yourself, understand that the world wants to shame you for that, but in the medical community, you would never deny a diabetic his insulin."[48] O'Hara eventually decided to try antidepressants and found that they helped her regain the ability to live her life normally even when she encountered one of her PTSD triggers. Each individual must speak with their own doctors to evaluate the treatment path that is right for them.

Having a Healthy Relationship

Many people who have been in an abusive relationship do not feel as though they are able to have—or deserve to have—a healthy relationship. They may believe, based on things they have seen in the media or heard from loved ones, that the abuse they encountered was simply the way things are in normal relationships. They may also have been conditioned by their abuser to believe this or to think that no one would ever want to have a healthy relationship with them.

In reality, healthy relationships are more common and more achievable than many people think, but they also do not look like many of the relationships people are used to seeing in the media or hearing about in songs. Media that is meant for entertainment often needs some kind of drama or conflict to drive a plot, so many stories revolve around unhealthy relationships because some people believe healthy relationships appear boring from the outside. However, as Holly Riordan wrote for *Thought Catalog*,

> *The best relationships are boring, because they're healthy. Because they're free from drama.*
>
> *Toxic relationships might seem fun at first, because they're wild and spontaneous and unpredictable. But they'll destroy you in the end. The lows they give you aren't worth the highs ...*

There's nothing better than a boring relationship. Because even though you'll spend large chunks of time grocery shopping and sharing silence, there will still be days when you kiss each other like it's the very first time. When you take a trip abroad and experience new cultures together. When you keep each other up all night laughing.

Boring relationships are the best relationships, because even when you should be bored, you don't feel bored. You feel happy. You feel like you're exactly where you're meant to be.[49]

Happy, healthy relationships often look boring from the outside, but they do not feel boring to the people who are in them.

Some characteristics of a healthy relationship include:

- Both partners understand that they are the only ones responsible for their own happiness. They do not rely on their partner to change their mood or be the source of all their joy in life.
- Both partners respect each other's boundaries. When there is conflict, they discuss it as calmly as possible, come to a mutually satisfactory solution, and then stop talking about it unless the issue comes up again.

- Each person has an equal voice in the relationship. Decisions that affect both people are not made without the input of both parties.
- Feelings are shared openly and are respected, not mocked or belittled.
- Both partners enjoy spending time with each other; it does not feel like a chore to speak to each other or schedule time to be with each other.
- As much as they enjoy spending time together, both partners also enjoy doing things on their own or with other friends, and neither resents the other for spending time apart.
- Neither person is using the other for something; they each appreciate the other for who they are as a person.

People who have been in an abusive relationship often feel frightened or confused in a healthy relationship. They may be waiting for their partner to turn abusive, or there may be things that happen in the new relationship that trigger old feelings. In one example, a teen named Valerie described how worried she was when she and her new girlfriend, Lisa, had their first fight:

> I didn't know what to do. I knew I'd be late, but I couldn't reach Lisa to tell her. I thought she'd be so mad, and I was scared because of how my last girlfriend used to attack me over every little thing. Lisa was mad, and worried, and she told me how mad she was. But she also listened and believed me when I explained what happened. It was over in a minute![50]

A healthy relationship does not mean a relationship that is forever free of any kind of conflict. Even the happiest couples fight. Instead, it is the way conflict is handled that determines whether a relationship is healthy. In a loving relationship, couples fight by explaining their own feelings calmly, staying on topic instead of bringing up past fights, trying to understand the other person's point of view, and working to come to a solution that meets both people's needs.

Although healthy relationships are achievable, abusive relationships are still a reality for many people, and sometimes, despite a person's best efforts, they fall into one. However, no one should have to accept an abusive relationship—whether it is with a romantic partner, family member, or friend—as simply "the way things are." Regardless of what has happened in the past, it is possible for a person to have loving, healthy relationships.

Introduction: Understanding Abuse

1. Lundy Bancroft, *Why Does He Do That?: Inside the Minds of Angry and Controlling Men*. New York, NY: G.P. Putnam's Sons, 2002, p. 84.

2. Andrea Mathews, "When Is It Emotional Abuse?," *Psychology Today*, September 26, 2016. www.psychologytoday. com/blog/traversing-the-inner-terrain/201609/when-is-it-emotional-abuse.

Chapter 1: Physical Abuse

3. Bancroft, *Why Does He Do That?*, p. 19

4. Jennifer L. Truman, Ph.D., and Rachel E. Morgan, Ph.D., "Special Report: Nonfatal Domestic Violence, 2003–2012," U.S. Department of Justice, April 2014. www.bjs.gov/ content/pub/pdf/ndv0312.pdf.

5. Bancroft, *Why Does He Do That?*, pp. 45–46.

6. Quoted in Michael Rodden, "What About Men? Lies, Statistics … and Peddling Myths About Violence Against Women," *The Citizen*, December 11, 2013. www.thecitizen.org. au/articles/what-about-men-lies-statistics-and-peddling-myths-about-violence-against-women.

7. "Is This Abuse?: Types of Abuse," Love Is Respect, accessed on April 15, 2018. www.loveisrespect.org/is-this-abuse/ types-of-abuse/.

8. Bancroft, *Why Does He Do That?*, p. 35.

9. Bancroft, *Why Does He Do That?*, p. 34.

10. Bancroft, *Why Does He Do That?*, pp. 72–73.

11. "Florence + the Machine—Kiss with a Fist," YouTube video, posted by florencemachine, 2:09, November 25, 2009. www.youtube.com/watch?v=1SmxVCM39j4.

12. Michelle Bernard, "Rihanna and Chris Brown Are Proof that Domestic Violence Is Everyone's Business," *Washington Post*, February 11, 2013. www.washingtonpost.com/blogs/she-the-people/wp/2013/02/11/rihanna-and-chris-brown-are-proof-that-domestic-violence-is-everyones-business/?noredirect=on&utm_term=.90f3aae2b60e.

13. Quoted in Bernard, "Rihanna and Chris Brown Are Proof that Domestic Violence Is Everyone's Business."

14. "Rihanna—We Found Love ft. Calvin Harris," YouTube video, posted by Rihanna, 4:35, October 19, 2011. www.youtube.com/watch?v=tg00YEETFzg.

15. Bancroft, *Why Does He Do That?*, pp. 147–148.

16. Quoted in Erin Reimel, "Nicole Kidman Wrote a Powerful Open Letter About Domestic Violence," *Glamour*, September 30, 2017. www.glamour.com/story/nicole-kidman-open-letter-domestic-violence-porter.

17. Sundi Rose, "25 of the Most Toxic Relationships on TV," *Culturess*, March 29, 2017. culturess.com/2017/03/29/25-toxic-relationships-tv-yes-faves/.

18. Quoted in Jennifer Arrow, "*Gossip Girl* Boss: 'Chuck Has Never, and Will Never, Hurt Blair,'" *E! News*, May 3, 2011. www.eonline.com/news/239902/gossip-girl-boss-chuck-has-never-and-will-never-hurt-blair.

19. Arrow, "*Gossip Girl* Boss."

Chapter 2: Emotional Abuse

20. Bancroft, *Why Does He Do That?*, p. 74.

21. Rachel Williams, "Spyware and Smartphones: How Abusive Men Track Their Partners," *The Guardian*, January 25, 2015. www.theguardian.com/lifeandstyle/2015/

jan/25/spyware-smartphone-abusive-men-track-partners-domestic-violence.

22. Williams, "Spyware and Smartphones."

23. Quoted in Williams, "Spyware and Smartphones."

24. Angela Guzman, "6 Signs of Emotional Abuse," Beliefnet, accessed on May 20, 2018. www.beliefnet.com/wellness/galleries/6-signs-of-emotional-abuse.aspx?p=2.

25. Stephanie A. Sarkis, Ph.D., "11 Warning Signs of Gaslighting," *Psychology Today*, January 22, 2017. www.psychology-today.com/us/blog/here-there-and-everywhere/201701/11-warning-signs-gaslighting.

26. Darlene Lancer, "How to Know if You're a Victim of Gaslighting," *Psychology Today*, January 13, 2018. www.psychology-today.com/us/blog/toxic-relationships/201801/how-know-if-youre-victim-gaslighting.

27. Bancroft, *Why Does He Do That?*, p. 86.

28. Bancroft, *Why Does He Do That?*, p. 118.

29. Sophie Brown, "Using *Twilight* to Educate About Abusive Relationships," *Wired*, January 25, 2011. www.wired.com/2011/01/using-twilight-to-educate-about-abusive-relationships/.

Chapter 3: Unhealthy Behaviors and Red Flags

30. Gavin de Becker, *The Gift of Fear: Survival Signals that Protect Us from Violence*. Boston, MA: Little, Brown and Company, 1997, p. 55.

31. De Becker, *The Gift of Fear*, p. 4.

32. Jennifer Peepas, "The Art of 'No,' Continued: Saying No When You've Already Said Yes," *Captain Awkward*, March 24, 2011. captainawkward.com/2011/03/24/the-art-of-no-continued-saying-no-when-youve-already-said-yes/.

33. De Becker, *The Gift of Fear*, pp. 59–60.

34. Nathan Thompson, "Confessions of an Ex-Pickup Artist," *Vice*, July 28, 2014. www.vice.com/en_us/article/gq89b4/confessions-of-a-teenage-pick-up-artist-865.

35. Thompson, "Confessions of an Ex-Pickup Artist."

36. Thompson, "Confessions of an Ex-Pickup Artist."

37. Lindsay Brown, "How to Spot a Pickup Artist," *Coveteur*, August 18, 2015. coveteur.com/2015/08/18/pickup-artist-tinder-in-brooklyn/.

38. "8 Pick Up Artist Techniques You Need to Master," PUA Training, June 5, 2017. www.puatraining.com/blog/pick-up-artist-techniques-you-need-to-master.

39. Bancroft, *Why Does He Do That?*, p. 119.

40. Bancroft, *Why Does He Do That?*, p. 115.

41. Bancroft, *Why Does He Do That?*, pp. 120–121.

Chapter 4: Dealing with Abuse

42. Quoted in Kelsey Borresen, "11 Subtle Signs You Might Be in an Abusive Relationship," *Huffington Post*, March 5, 2018. www.huffingtonpost.com/entry/signs-of-emotional-abuse-relationship_us_5a999fbee4b0a0ba4ad31a4d.

43. Barrie Levy, *In Love and in Danger: A Teen's Guide to Breaking Free of Abusive Relationships*. Berkeley, CA: Seal Press, 2006, p. 106.

44. Marian Betancourt, *What to Do When Love Turns Violent: A Practical Resource for Women in Abusive Relationships*. Bloomington, IN: iUniverse, 2009, pp. 38–39.

45. "History of the Violence Against Women Act," Legal Momentum, accessed on June 17, 2018. www.legalmomentum.org/history-vawa.

Chapter 5: Recovering from Abuse

46. "Complex PTSD," PTSD: National Center for PTSD,

last updated February 23, 2016. www.ptsd.va.gov/professional/ptsd-overview/complex-ptsd.asp.

47. Mary Emily O'Hara, "Meds Don't Make Women Crazy—Trauma Does," *Daily Beast*, April 10, 2015. www.thedailybeast.com/meds-dont-make-women-crazytrauma-does.

48. Quoted in Sierra Marquina, "Kristen Bell Opens Up About Struggle with Anxiety and Depression: 'The World Wants to Shame You,'" *Us Weekly*, May 6, 2016. www.usmagazine.com/celebrity-news/news/kristen-bell-reveals-she-takes-prescription-for-anxiety-and-depression-w205585.

49. Holly Riordan, "The Best Relationships Are Boring," *Thought Catalog*, June 12, 2017. thoughtcatalog.com/holly-riordan/2017/06/the-best-relationships-are-boring/.

50. Quoted in Levy, *In Love and in Danger*, p. 109.

DISCUSSION QUESTIONS

Chapter 1: Physical Abuse

1. Why do you think people ask why someone does not leave an abusive relationship rather than asking why someone would be abusive?

2. What are some types of relationships that can have a power imbalance aside from heterosexual romantic ones?

3. Can you think of reasons why someone might stay in an abusive relationship aside from the ones given in this chapter?

Chapter 2: Emotional Abuse

1. Are there any behaviors discussed in this chapter that you were surprised to see described as emotional abuse? Why do you think people have such a difficult time identifying emotionally abusive behavior?

2. Find a partner, and act out a disagreement between the two of you on an issue such as where to go for dinner. You can also imagine the disagreement if a partner is not available. What are some healthy ways the disagreement can be resolved?

3. What are some movies, TV shows, songs, or other media that present emotional abuse as loving behavior? How has watching or listening to these shaped your view of romantic relationships?

Chapter 3: Unhealthy Behaviors and Red Flags

1. Can you think of characteristics of toxic relationships that were not discussed in the book?

2. Describe a time when you felt uncomfortable around someone but were not immediately sure why. Can you identify what made you uneasy?

3. Do you think "You're not like other girls" is a compliment? Why or why not?

Chapter 4: Dealing with Abuse

1. What are some things not mentioned in this chapter that a person needs to include in their safety plan when trying to leave an abusive relationship?

2. Why is telling someone about abuse important?

3. If a friend told you they were being abused, what would you do?

Chapter 5: Recovering from Abuse

1. Why might an abuse survivor feel uncomfortable in a healthy relationship?

2. Why is therapy an important part of recovering from an abusive relationship?

3. Describe what you think a healthy relationship looks like.

Love Is Respect

call: (866) 331-9474

text: loveis to 22522

www.loveisrespect.org

> Love Is Respect, a project by the National Domestic Violence Hotline, is aimed at helping young adults. Its website features a live chat as well as articles about abuse, quizzes such as "Am I a Good Partner?" and "Is My Relationship Healthy?," and advice on how to get help. The website offers a warning about computer monitoring and a "quick escape" button to exit the website immediately. People who think their online activity may be monitored should access the website at a trusted friend's house or at a library.

Naseeha Youth Helpline

240 Superior Blvd

Suite 214

Mississauga, Ontario

L5T 2L2

(866) 627-3342

naseeha.org

> This organization, which operates a helpline on weeknights from 6:00 p.m. to 9:00 p.m. Eastern Standard Time, is aimed at helping Muslim youths, who may face unique religious or cultural challenges on issues such as bullying, mental health, and abuse.

National Domestic Violence Hotline

PO Box 161810

Austin, TX 78716

(800) 799-7233

www.thehotline.org

> This hotline, which operates 24 hours a day, 7 days a week, connects callers with trained advocates who can help them identify abuse, offer support and advice, and connect them with local resources. The website also has a live chat option and information about the difference between abusive and healthy relationships. Like Love Is Respect, this website also offers a warning about computer monitoring and a "quick escape" button.

National Network to End Domestic Violence (NNEDV)

1325 Massachusetts Avenue NW, 7th Floor

Washington, DC 20005

(202) 543-5566

nnedv.org

> This nonprofit organization is committed to bringing attention to the issue of domestic violence and changing the way society views it.

National Suicide Prevention Lifeline

(800) 273-8255

suicidepreventionlifeline.org

> Ongoing abuse can make someone depressed enough to believe that suicide is the only way out, especially if they feel as though they have no one to turn to. However, suicide is never the answer to a person's problems, and help is available. This hotline is available for anyone in the United States dealing with severe emotional distress or suicidal thoughts, and it can be called 24 hours a day, 7 days a week.

Rape, Abuse, and Incest National Network (RAINN)

(800) 656-4673

www.rainn.org

> This organization, whose website includes a live chat, can offer advice and support for survivors of domestic or sexual abuse, including information about national and local laws, referrals for courtroom advocates, and help finding a local health facility that is trained in treating abuse victims.

Books

Bancroft, Lundy. *Why Does He Do That?: Inside the Minds of Angry and Controlling Men*. New York, NY: G.P. Putnam's Sons, 2002.
> Bancroft draws on his experience counseling abusive men to explain the types of abusers, their thought processes, the tactics they use, and myths about abuse.

Betancourt, Marian. *What to Do When Love Turns Violent: A Practical Resource for Women in Abusive Relationships*. Bloomington, IN: iUniverse, 2009.
> This book gives advice for abused women on topics such as what evidence to bring to court, how to protect themselves and their children after leaving the relationship, how to find emergency shelter, and how to begin rebuilding their life after the abuse is over.

Dessen, Sarah. *Dreamland*. New York, NY: Penguin Group, 2000.
> It can be hard for people to imagine the ways abusive behaviors can show up and the various ways they can be combined. This novel documents an abusive relationship from beginning to end, showing how a person can get sucked in and why it can be difficult for them to leave.

Gitlin, Martin. *Helping a Friend in an Abusive Relationship*. New York, NY: Rosen Publishing, 2017.
> This book is a resource for young adults who have a friend in an abusive relationship. It provides information about identifying abuse, ways to support a victim of abuse, and organizations that can provide help for both the victim and their friends.

Levy, Barrie. *In Love and in Danger: A Teen's Guide to Breaking Free of Abusive Relationships*. Berkeley, CA: Seal Press, 2006.
> This book, which addresses teens' unique concerns and gives stories from real teenage abuse survivors, explains how to recognize abuse and how to safely leave an abusive relationship. It also includes a chapter for abusers who want to change their behavior and a safety plan worksheet at the back of the book.

Websites

Break the Cycle

breakthecycle.org

> This organization gives information about what an abusive relationship is and ways people can help friends as well as get involved in raising awareness about abuse in teen relationships.

iPrevail

www.iprevail.com

> Seeking help from a therapist is an important step in recovering from an abusive relationship, but many people have difficulty accessing affordable mental health care. The website iPrevail, which is also available as an app for iPhone and Android, allows people to chat about their problems for free with a trained, unlicensed listener. For $9.99 per month, the user can access licensed therapists. Always ask a parent or guardian before purchasing a subscription.

Scarleteen

scarleteen.com

> This website focuses primarily on comprehensive sexual education, but several articles and answers to reader-submitted questions deal with the issues of domestic violence and psychological abuse. Additionally, the website offers information about how to build a healthy romantic relationship in all aspects.

Teen Dating Violence Awareness Month

www.teendvmonth.org

> This is the official website of Teen Dating Violence Awareness Month, which takes place every February to increase understanding of abusive relationships among teens and what can be done to help victims of teen dating violence.

#ThatsNotLove

joinonelove.org/act/thats-not-love

> This website was created to help young adults identify unhealthy relationship behaviors. The short movies on the website explore 10 unhealthy behaviors to help people recognize them in their own life, and other resources are also provided to help people learn and teach others about healthy and unhealthy relationships.

INDEX

PICTURE CREDITS

ABOUT THE AUTHOR

Jennifer Lombardo earned her BA in English from the University at Buffalo and still resides in Buffalo, New York, with her cat, Chip. She has helped write a number of books for young adults on topics ranging from world history to body image. In her spare time, she enjoys cross-stitching, hiking, and volunteering with local organizations. She is passionate about helping people recognize the signs of abuse and firmly believes that healthy relationships can be achieved.